Praise for the First Edition

"Pick it up for its emphasis on self-acceptance and its A-to-Z nature."
—**Scholastic Parent & Child**

"[T]he authors lay a strong foundation in giving kids the ultimate skill of self-advocacy."
—**Booklist**

"Useful and easily readable . . . with lots of practical advice."
—**Kirkus Reviews**

"Should be one of the first books a family buys after a diagnosis . . .
it will be invaluable to so many children and their families."
—**Claire LaZebnik, author of *Things I Should Have Known* and *Growing Up on the Spectrum***

THE SURVIVAL GUIDE FOR
Kids with
Autism Spectrum Disorder
(And Their Parents)

UPDATED EDITION

Elizabeth Verdick & Elizabeth Reeve, M.D.

Illustrated by Nick Kobyluch

free spirit
PUBLISHING®

T0034991

Library of Congress Cataloging-in-Publication Data
Names: Verdick, Elizabeth, author. | Reeve, Elizabeth, author.
Title: The survival guide for kids with autism spectrum disorder (and their parents) / Elizabeth Verdick, Elizabeth Reeve, M.D.
Description: Updated edition. | Minneapolis : Free Spirit Publishing, [2021] |
    Includes bibliographical references and index. | Audience: Ages 9–13
Identifiers: LCCN 2020026008 (print) | LCCN 2020026009 (ebook) | ISBN 9781631985997 (paperback) | ISBN 9781631986000 (pdf) | ISBN 9781631986017 (epub)
Subjects: LCSH: Children with autism spectrum disorders—Juvenile literature. | Autistic children—Family relationships—Juvenile literature. | Parents of autistic children—Juvenile literature.
Classification: LCC RJ506.A9 V466 2021 (print) | LCC RJ506.A9 (ebook) | DDC 618.92/85882—dc23
LC record available at https://lccn.loc.gov/2020026008
LC ebook record available at https://lccn.loc.gov/2020026009

Free Spirit Publishing does not have control over or assume responsibility for author or third-party websites and their content. At the time of this book's publication, all facts and figures cited within are the most current available. All telephone numbers, addresses, and website URLs are accurate and active as of September 2020. If you find an error or believe that a resource listed here is not as described, please contact Free Spirit Publishing. Parents, teachers, and other adults: We strongly urge you to monitor children's use of the internet.

Note: The names of some children described in this book have been changed to protect their privacy.

Edited by Marjorie Lisovskis
Cover and interior design by Michelle Lee Lagerroos and Shannon Pourciau

All illustrations by Nick Kobyluch, except illustrations on pages 11 (rainbow), 20, 21, 34, 36, 45, 61, 62, 67 (calendar), 70, 77, 99, 100, 141, 145 (pencil and books), 151, 166, 168, 229 by Michelle Lee Lagerroos and Shannon Pourciau
Photo on page 32 © istockphoto.com/Leontura
Photo on page 33 © Rosalie Winard

Printed by: 70548
Printed in: China
PO#: 9739

Free Spirit Publishing
An imprint of Teacher Created Materials
9850 51st Avenue North, Suite 100
Minneapolis, MN 55442
(612) 338-2068
help4kids@freespirit.com
freespirit.com

FSC
www.fsc.org
MIX
Paper | Supporting
responsible forestry
FSC® C144853

Dedication

To Nancy, Cara, and Trish: You were there in the beginning and you helped bring us further than we imagined possible. Forever grateful, EV

To all the patients and families I have worked with over the past 30 years. You have each taught me something! ER

Acknowledgments

For their careful and thoughtful reviews of the manuscript for this book, thanks go to Cindy Kaldor, autism behavior consultant for the Osseo School District; Kim Klein, Ph.D., pediatric neuropsychologist with Fraser Child and Family Center; Amy Nygaard, attending child and adolescent psychiatrist at Regions Behavioral Health, Woodbury, Minnesota; Pat Pulice, director of Fraser Autism Services; Linda Sieford, Ph.D., family and educational consultant and adjunct faculty in psychology; Angela Henchen; Mary Stefanski; and Daniel Stefanski.

We also send out a huge thank you to all the kids, teens, moms, and dads who took the time to tell us their thoughts about life on the spectrum.

Contents

Part 1
A Look into Autism Spectrum Disorder

Part 2 Home, School, Community

Part 3 Body and Brain Basics

Introduction for Kids

Have you ever sensed you're different somehow? Maybe you don't seem to fit in with the kids at school or in your neighborhood. You look around and see them talking, laughing, messaging, and living life at a different speed than you are. Perhaps you even feel out of step within your own family.

Or, maybe you don't feel so different but other kids treat you as if you are. They may tease you, stare, shy away from you, or tell on you for behaving in ways you didn't even know were "wrong." What's going on? You're special in some way, but how?

This book is about discovering why you're different. Like many people, you have some special skills and gifts. But you also have some special needs. More specifically, you have a condition known as autism spectrum disorder, or ASD. The definition on the next page will explain it more.

1

ASD—What Do These Initials Mean?

ASD is the short and simple way to say **autism spectrum disorder.** But ASD is far from simple.

You probably noticed that the word *autism* is part of ASD. So, what is autism? Doctors and other professionals use this word to describe brain disorders that affect how you think, learn, communicate, and behave.

The word *spectrum* in autism spectrum disorder means "wide range." This is a good word to use because the term *autism* can describe a wide range of different symptoms. All people with autism have some type of difficulty with:

- communication
- social skills
- how they enjoy activities and interests

These difficulties may be mild or more serious—and every person with autism is unique. People with autism have a "spectrum" of differences.

Because people with the symptoms of autism are now mainly referred to as being "on the spectrum," we use that language in this book. We talk about **autism, autism spectrum disorder,** and **ASD.** We like to use phrases like "kids with autism" rather than "kids who are autistic" or "autistic kids." Some people use terms like "autistic person" freely. Others don't. We used language we prefer—hope that's A-OK with you!

In the past, other terms were sometimes used to describe people on the spectrum. Maybe you've heard of "Asperger's" or "Asperger's syndrome." This term applied to those who had the symptoms of autism but who didn't have difficulties in learning to talk or in the speed of their learning when they were young. The word *Asperger's* comes from Johann ("Hans") Asperger, a doctor who studied mental disorders in children in the 1930s and 1940s. Today, doctors and other experts do not use his name to describe people with ASD—they use the term "autism spectrum disorder."

If you've been diagnosed with Asperger's in the past and prefer that term, that's fine too. Lots of people still use it. In fact, if you turn to "Where to Go for More Info" (pages 233–234), you'll see book titles about Asperger's and "Aspies." *Aspie* is a short form, a nickname. You're free to use whatever term you like to describe *you*.

Learning that you have ASD can be a confusing experience—and we'd like to make it easier for you. We want to tell you "It's going to be okay." And it *is.* That doesn't mean it's going to be "super simple" or "problem free," though. We wish it could be. But life is hardly ever super simple and problem free.

We wrote this book to help you better understand your needs and differences. We hope it will help you with daily issues, such as your feelings, behavior, and communication with other people. We recommend that you read the book with an adult, even if you're already a strong reader. Why? Because reading with a parent or another grown-up who cares about you is an important way to get support. An adult can answer your questions and help you try out the ideas and tips.

Another reason we wrote this book is because we have a special place in our hearts for kids who have ASD. Both of us are mothers whose sons are on the spectrum. While raising our sons, we've heard comments like:

> *"People with autism can't live in the 'real' world—*
> *they're in their own little world."*

or

> *"People with ASD never have many friends or want to be social."*

We don't believe in can't or never. If you have ASD, there are some differences between you and other people. But your life can be about *can.* You *can*

- make friends
- succeed to the best of your ability in school
- be an awesome son, daughter, sister, brother, or friend
- learn, grow, and connect with others

Never say never. Life is about trying your best and learning from each new experience. We believe in you and want you to grow up healthy, strong, and proud of who you are! The power to do that is in your hands—with help from your family, your school, and the experts you work with.

Let this book help you along the way. We know it's a long book. But learning about ASD and facing its challenges can be a long process— one that takes time and effort. The book is not meant to be read all at once. Use it in a way that works for you, focusing on chapters or sections that are useful at a given time. Think of it as a handbook you can go to when you need help with a certain issue or have a question about ASD. You and your parents can turn to it again and again over the years.

The table of contents and the index can guide you to topics of interest. Look at the stories of kids with autism: you may find inspiration or shared experiences. Try some of the book's tips to see what helps you right now. But remember that learning new skills takes time, patience, and practice. Give yourself the time you need.

If you have questions that the book doesn't answer or if you want to tell us about yourself, email us at: help4kids@freespirit.com. We can't wait to hear from you!

Elizabeth & Elizabeth

P.S. On the next page is a section for adults, written for any grown-ups who are reading this book with you. If you'd like, you can go straight to Chapter 1 (page 10) to find out more about the question "What Is ASD?"

Introduction
for Adults

*"If you've met one person with autism,
you've met one person with autism."*

What a great quote. It's often repeated, and for good reason—people with autism spectrum disorder are complex and unique. They're *individuals*. They can't all be lumped together, because there are vast differences in how they think, learn, feel, behave, and communicate. It's why this popular quote is important for parents, educators, doctors, and experts to always keep in mind.

Sometimes autism is referred to as an invisible disability. In other words, the person isn't in a wheelchair or may not have an obvious physical impairment—so people might assume there's nothing different, nothing "wrong." But autism does affect how someone communicates, socializes, and learns. People with autism spectrum disorder (ASD) behave differently from what is considered "typical" or *neurotypical* (a term sometimes preferred by the autism community; it means "neurologically normal"). Someone with autism isn't typical, yet the person cannot be defined only in terms of the diagnosis.

You're probably reading this book because someone you love (or teach) has autism spectrum disorder. You want to help. Chances are, this young person in your life is now old enough to begin learning about the diagnosis. *The Survival Guide for Kids with Autism Spectrum Disorder (And Their Parents)* is a handbook to help children through the questions, challenges, frustrations, tears, mysteries, successes—the journey. We recommend this book mainly for kids ages eight to thirteen, although older kids may also find it useful. Depending on age and ability, some children may be able to read the book independently. However, we suggest that you and the child share and discuss it together. Even a child who is an adept reader will benefit from having a grown-up read alongside for support, empathy, and further explanation of the issues discussed. As a parent, you may also find that reading together is a chance to strengthen your relationship with your child and keep the door open to questions and issues that arise.

This book is designed to help a child with ASD through many ages and stages, from learning about the diagnosis to facing physical and emotional challenges to improving communication and social skills at home, at school, and in the wider world. Use the book as an everyday tool or guide, or as a way to introduce a new topic or skill. You may find it helpful to come back to the book during times when the child is asking questions, facing changes at home or school, reaching a milestone, or struggling. Because children grow and change—and because their ASD changes too—they need a book that keeps them informed and helps them achieve to the best of their abilities and at their own pace.

As you may know, the autism community is growing larger by the day. More kids are being diagnosed, more parents are becoming advocates, and more educators are being trained to understand the autism spectrum. There are many voices, many points of view—so many stories of hardship and hope. And we've been a part of the story ourselves. Both of us are mothers of sons who have autism, and one of us is a doctor who works with children and adults with autism spectrum disorder. At times, the two of us wondered how this one book could possibly meet the needs of such a wide and varied audience of passionate, questioning advocates.

In the end, we kept coming back to these questions: What do the *kids* need? What are *their* issues, questions, and experiences? We wrote this book to help kids with autism spectrum disorder get answers to the questions that are important to them, learn more about issues they struggle with, and find out what it's like for other kids who have ASD.

The Survival Guide is divided into three parts:

- **Part 1: A Look into Autism Spectrum Disorder** is a kids' primer on the symptoms, the sensory issues, famous people with the condition, questions that arise, and building a team of helpers.

- **Part 2: Home, School, Community** is about improving daily life at home, at school, and in the wider world. We want kids and families to know that everything you do can make a difference. Some days, you may want to give up, or you'll think "This is just too hard" and "Why even try?" Daily life with ASD can be frustrating—but it also can be full of great humor, acceptance, and gratitude for the little things. Part 2 offers tips for making everyday life easier, as well as for setting short- and long-term goals for improving social skills or school performance. What you do for your child matters. Our aim with Part 2 is to help both your child and you keep moving forward, even when it's hard to do.

- **Part 3: Body and Brain Basics** looks into the physical and emotional issues that are such a big part of life with ASD. Readers will learn about exercise, nutrition, sleep, relaxation, handling intense emotions, and more. Here we emphasize the importance of good self-care—because it's a huge step toward better health and greater confidence.

All three parts of the book contain real-life stories of kids with autism spectrum disorder (names and details have been changed to protect their privacy).

These stories give a glimpse into the range of challenges our children face each day. The book also includes quotes from real kids who have shared thoughts and insights that may help others with ASD realize they're not alone.

After Part 3, you'll find additional information for you and your child, including a section for parents and caregivers called "Sharing the Diagnosis with Your Child." We hope it helps you feel more confident about—and ready for—this special conversation.

Your role as a parent is unique and complex, just as your child is unique and complex. You need added support from relatives, friends, neighbors, teachers, therapists, doctors, experts, and local organizations focused on autism spectrum disorder. If you're struggling to juggle all that's required of you, ask for help. Even if you're not struggling, ask for help. Reaching out can be an enlightening, rewarding experience. You'll likely find a community of people with amazing stories, invaluable knowledge, strong bonds, and exceptional openness and tolerance.

Being a parent to a special-needs child takes a unique kind of knowledge, courage, and dedication. There's no map to point the way—no expert who can tell you exactly what's best for your child now or in the future. You'll learn by trying new things, seeing what works and what doesn't, and gathering all the support and resources you can. Autism spectrum disorder teaches you. Your child teaches you. Other families living with ASD teach you. Together, you and your child grow stronger with every new challenge you face.

We wrote this book because we care a lot about young people on the spectrum. We believe they can succeed at home, at school, and in their communities. We want them to enjoy life, set goals within their reach, make friends, keep friends, learn, grow, achieve, know who they are, and feel a sense of belonging in the world. We hope to give readers (both young and not so young) a sense of optimism and positive direction. However, we're not suggesting that you should be relentlessly upbeat about your child's condition or expect miracles—after all, autism spectrum disorder is a very real and challenging condition. Let's put it this way: Don't think of ASD as a life sentence . . . it's a life difference. People with autism spectrum disorder can have rich, fulfilling lives.

You teach them how. You lead the way. Let this book be one of the many tools you turn to for help on the journey.

For more information, we recommend looking into the Autism Society: autism-society.org. You can also check out the American Academy of Child and Adolescent Psychiatry at aacap.org (search for autism) or visit the autism section of the Mayo Clinic's website: mayoclinic.org.

Part 1

A look into Autism Spectrum Disorder

Chapter 1

What Is ASD?

ASD stands for autism spectrum disorder. But *disorder* isn't a very friendly word. If you want, you can think of ASD as a brain difference.

Because the difference starts in the brain, ASD has an effect on your body too. Your brain is like your command center. It sends billions of messages 24/7 to all areas of your body. Messages like:

"Legs, run!"   "Hey, what's that noise?"

"Ouch, that bright sun hurts my eyes."

"Mmmm, I smell lunch. Time to eat."

Your brain plays an important role in three areas having to do with autism spectrum disorder:

1. **Communication:** This is about how you listen, speak, write, or get messages across to others.

2. **Socialization:** *Socializing* is doing things with other people. Your brain affects how you socialize with others and how much you want to socialize with them. It affects how you fit into a group, like your family, friends, or community.

3. **Interests and behaviors:** Interests are the things you think about and the activities you enjoy. Behaviors are the things you do and how you act. Your brain plays a role in how often you think or do things, and how much you enjoy them.

If you have ASD, your brain has to work harder when it comes to communicating and socializing. All this hard work might make you feel tired or frustrated, but you can do it! This book will tell you how.

On pages 16–24, you'll learn more about each of the three key areas mentioned above. But first, a word about rainbows . . .

The Many Colors of ASD

Rainbows? What do rainbows have to do with the autism spectrum? You might have seen the word *spectrum* if you've read about rainbows. The spectrum refers to the colors of light in a rainbow (red, orange, yellow, green, blue, indigo, and violet). Just like the rainbow, autism comes in many colors, including your special color! The "spectrum" part of ASD means that each and every person with this condition is different and unique.

ASD and Y-O-U

Maybe your doctor and parents (or caregivers) have explained your condition to you already. Or maybe they're still in the process of figuring things out. Coming up with the diagnosis of ASD takes time.

To do so, your doctor looks at your medical history, your habits and behaviors, and information about you from your school. Lots of questions come up, like:

- How do you communicate?
- What are your interests?
- How do you play?
- Do you have friends? How do you get along together?
- How do you do in school?
- What do you like to eat?
- What are your sleeping habits?
- Do you have trouble handling your feelings?

To understand you even better, the doctor takes your answers to the questions and compares them to the list of autism symptoms (problems) in a special book.* This can be tricky because every person with autism is so unique. The "magic number" of symptoms the doctor looks for is five. A person with ASD must have at least five symptoms that include difficulties with:

You might have more than five symptoms— that's okay too.

- communication
- socialization
- limited interests and/or repetitive behaviors

Your doctor will also take a look at your childhood history, especially at what age you learned to speak. Some kids who have a diagnosis of autism had a hard time learning to talk

---

*The book is called *The Diagnostic and Statistical Manual of Mental Disorders Fifth Edition* (or *DSM-5*).

when they were young. They may have been late to start talking, and might have needed speech therapy to start getting the words out. Some people with autism never learn how to speak. They may use special communication tools.

Sam's Story

Sam is 10 years old and has autism. He looks like any other 10-year-old boy—unless something exciting is happening. Then Sam starts rocking back and forth in his chair and flapping his arms like a baby bird ready for its first flight. This is one of the things Sam doesn't like about his autism—he can't keep himself from "flapping" when he's happy or excited.

When Sam was younger, the kids at school didn't seem to mind his flapping. But now that he's older, the kids don't seem as accepting of his behaviors. These days, he feels really embarrassed when he flaps.

Another problem for Sam at school is his voice. People say he talks too loud. His teacher reminds him to use his "indoor voice." Sam tries to talk more softly, but this only lasts a short time. Pretty soon he's speaking loudly again, and he gets the same reminder about using his indoor voice.

Sometimes Sam feels sad or frustrated about what's hard for him. Then he tries to stop and think about the good things in his life. Sam is the best speller in his class, and he has lots of energy and enthusiasm. He loves to learn new things, and he knows more knock-knock jokes than anyone else in his whole school! Many kids at school and in Sam's neighborhood know him, and they always say hello. All of this makes Sam feel better about himself.

For now, he thinks, maybe a little flapping and loud talking aren't so bad—especially when he thinks of all the good things in his life.

ASD Is Not . . .

- your fault
- something you "caught" like a germ
- something you can "give others" (autism is not contagious)
- a sign that you are stupid, bad, sick, crazy, lazy, flawed, or weird

ASD Is . . .

A medical condition. You have symptoms, but with help from experts, family members, and teachers, you can work on improving those symptoms. ASD is also a way of being—it's how you experience the world.

You may have ASD, but you're still you. You're a whole person, head to toe, inside and out. You have the potential to live a healthy, unique, and remarkable life.

I have what some people would call a disability but I call a gift. . . . I am not your average child. I like to think of myself as the 'new and improved model.'

—Luke Jackson, from his book *Freaks, Geeks & Asperger Syndrome*

Chapter 2

Symptoms of ASD

In many ways, autism spectrum disorder is a mystery. There's no simple test (like a blood test) to show that a person has autism. Instead, it's a matter of looking for symptoms and seeing whether they match up with the diagnosis of ASD.

This chapter is all about understanding the symptoms you may have. You can imagine that you're a detective, looking for clues to the mystery. Detectives almost always have partners. Ask a parent or another adult you trust to study the clues with you, so you can figure out things together.

Detectives take good notes. Get a pen or pencil and some paper. Whenever you read about a symptom that sounds familiar, write it down. These notes are clues about areas you might need help with.

Symptom 1:
Communication Difficulties

Most people with autism spectrum disorder can talk, although it may be hard for them to find the right words to express what they want to say. Do you ever feel like other people are watching you too closely or hurrying you to say something? Or do you sometimes use words that are correct but sound odd to your friends? Sometimes, you might have trouble understanding what others are saying. Maybe it seems like they talk too fast. Perhaps they tell jokes that don't seem funny to you, or use slang words you haven't heard before.

Some people who have ASD may misunderstand common expressions. For example, you might hear your mom say she's "fed up" and think she's full from eating too much. But what "fed up" really means is *frustrated.* Or, someone might say "Take a hike." You might think the person means "Put on some hiking boots and find the nearest trail." The expression "Take a hike" said in an annoyed tone of voice usually means "Go away!"

Understanding words that you read may also be hard, even if you love reading! Some people with ASD are super spellers and fast readers but may have trouble making sense of the story or information. Do you sometimes read a section nearly perfectly, even when it's full of long words? And then find that you're unable to explain to someone else what you just read? If so, this is because your brain is good at decoding (figuring out) the *sounds* of words, but not their *meanings.*

Problems understanding the meaning of language happen when parts of your brain don't communicate with each other. Think of it this way: Part of your brain has the job of making words. Another part has the job of understanding feelings. Both parts of your brain may be doing their jobs—but they're not talking to each other! Messages are lost along the way or take a while to get there.

Because of your ASD, your brain tends to focus on one thing at a time. For example, imagine someone is angry at you. That person may look something like the girl at the top of the next page.

Your brain might not see the "whole picture" that someone without ASD sees. What do you see instead? *Pieces* of the picture. You may hear an angry voice but not be able to focus on what the words mean. You may see an angry face but not notice the person shaking her foot. You may be focused on listening for words, and then miss the person's facial expression.

People use a combination of words, actions, and facial expressions to let others know what they think and feel. For you, it's harder to see, hear, and understand that combination.

When your brain doesn't see the whole picture right away, you have to put the pieces together bit by bit. You might not realize at first that the person is angry at you. Or you may notice the person is mad but not understand why. It's almost like someone is talking to you in a different language. You hear the words and you see the person's mouth move, but it takes you longer to figure out what's being said.

Then there's the communication that happens without any words. You might not notice people's gestures, like when they wave, wink, roll their eyes, or tap their foot. Or you might misunderstand someone's body language. For example, if someone elbows you in the ribs, you might think, "Hey, he's bothering me!" But maybe the person didn't mean to bother you at all. Maybe he was trying, without words, to get you to notice something interesting or funny.

Having ASD might mean your brain has a slower "processing speed." So, you can think interesting thoughts, but then have a hard time putting them into words. You might not be able to answer a question as quickly as you'd like. Or, you might have trouble organizing your thoughts when you have to write. These communication problems slow you down, but they don't mean you're not smart!

Sometimes you might get stuck on words. Maybe certain ones are special to you, and you repeat them again and again. Other times, you may feel the need to ask the same question over and over. You might do this even though you know the answer and the person has already replied to you lots of times. It's almost as if your brain has a hiccup. You can't control these brain hiccups, just like you can't control regular hiccups.

Take a Look!

This chapter is all about the three main types of symptoms of ASD. You'll find help for coping with all these symptoms later in the book, especially in chapters 10, 11, and 12.

Most likely, your family and friends get annoyed when you're repeating words or questions—even though you can't help it. This urge to repeat yourself just feels right to you, the same way it feels satisfying to scratch an itch. Then, just as suddenly as the urge started, it stops. It can feel like a big relief to you when you finally quit repeating yourself.

All sorts of communication issues come up with ASD. You may have some of the ones discussed here or other ones unique to you.

Symptom 2:
Problems with Social Skills

Social skills are something everyone has to learn within their own family, culture, and community. We're not born knowing exactly how to be social. But most people are born with a built-in ability to watch and copy the people around them.

Maybe you've seen how babies look closely at their parents and imitate motions like waving or clapping. Toddlers learn to nod their head for yes and shake their head for no. As they grow, young children learn other social skills. They learn to do things like say "please" and "thank you," or apologize if they've hurt someone.

Having ASD makes it harder to learn these everyday skills. Imitation doesn't come as easily to you. Remember, your brain tends to focus on one thing at a time. This affects your social skills because you don't always see the "whole picture" at once.

Because of your ASD, it might be hard for you to look people in the eye or to look at their faces when you talk. At times, you might try to look them in the eye and then forget what you wanted to say.

 Sometimes eye contact is hard. It's really easy to lose focus when I look people in the eye.

—12-year-old boy

The back-and-forth of conversation is probably difficult for you too. For example, you may find it fairly easy to talk about what interests you. But then you might forget to give the other person a chance to speak. Maybe you forget to ask questions, or find them hard to ask. Perhaps you have trouble following other people's conversations. Or maybe people tell you not to interrupt. Because of these difficulties, social situations are tougher for you. You might feel shy or misunderstood.

For everyone, a big part of being social is using their face, hands, or body to express themselves. ASD makes these things hard to do. You may not be able to easily understand the expression on someone's face, especially if it doesn't seem to match what the person is saying.

This difficulty with gestures and facial expressions might mean that you don't use much body language. Have people ever told you that you seem "like a robot" or have an odd tone of voice? Maybe you don't use your arms and hands much when you speak—instead, you stay still. Or maybe the expression on your face stays flat, not changing into a smile, a frown, or an angry look very often. You might speak in a *monotone,* meaning your tone doesn't change to show the feelings behind your words. You might not nod your head when you're listening to others speak. (Nodding can be a clue to tell others "I hear and understand you.")

These differences in how you interact with other people might confuse them. The good news is you can learn to use more gestures and expressions if you want to. The more you practice, the better you'll get at it.

Symptom 3:
Intense Interests and Repetitive Behaviors

If you have ASD, you probably also have some cool hobbies and interests. Kids with autism spectrum disorder often have intense interests, fascinations, and obsessions.

Maybe you know nearly everything there is to know about dinosaurs, presidents, or the planets in the solar system. When you're fascinated by something, you want to learn as much as you can about it. What's wrong with that? Nothing! Hobbies and activities give you something to do and help you discover more about the world.

You've probably heard of Pokémon. Maybe you even have Pokémon video games or toys. Pokémon is short for "pocket monster." Guess who came up with the idea for those little Pokémon characters? Satoshi Tajiri, who self-identifies as having ASD.

Satoshi was born in 1965 in a rural part of Tokyo. As a child, he was so fascinated by the insects he collected that other kids called him "Dr. Bug." He had trouble in school, and as a teen, he often cut class to go to the arcade. He played video games for hours, wanting to be the best. He eventually finished high school and earned a technical degree. Later, he founded a company called Game Freak.

Satoshi Tajiri's career and creations are fun to explore. Something that stands out is how he never lost his intense urge to collect and share. He wondered, what if *gamers* could gather creatures? Populate their own little worlds? Battle the creatures? Share them with other players? *Connect*, in other words. No one else had thought of that! Satoshi went from being a struggling student to a successful video game developer. Still, he faced hard times. He lost sleep. He lost money. He could have given up, but his mentors and friends believed in him. Remember Satoshi Tajiri if you find yourself questioning your own fascinations. Could they lead to something in the future?

It's great when your interests fit the interests of your friends and other people your age. Maybe you love video games that are popular with other kids, or you enjoy movies, collector cards, chess, or math. These activities give you an opportunity to make friends with people who share your interests. But sometimes, ASD leads to interests that are unusual and make it harder to have friends.

For example, what if you're fascinated by bus schedules or phone numbers? Or what if you have an obsession with sports statistics, even though you don't actually care much about the sport itself? Interests like these aren't bad—but you do them alone. They often involve a lot of memorizing, which you're probably good at, but they don't give you a way to relate to other people.

Maybe family members and friends often ask you to stop talking about a certain topic or to get a new activity. That's not easy to hear. You may be happy talking about the same thing or playing the same game for hours. But people who don't have ASD usually don't have your level of intensity. They like to talk about lots of different things. Sometimes they like to talk more than play. That's a social difference between people who have autism spectrum disorder and those who don't.

DeShawn's Story

DeShawn, who's 12, *loves* to take apart anything electronic. His friends gave him the nickname "Garbage Guy" just for fun, because his favorite activity is going to the junk store to buy old stuff to take apart. DeShawn spends hours each day looking through websites that sell electronics. He makes lists of all the things he wants to buy. He even has a special box in his room to store his favorite creations—things he's made from junk.

Sometimes DeShawn gets in trouble at home because he doesn't do his homework when he's supposed to. He forgets all about his homework when he's busy doing his electronics projects. And he's not that into homework anyway. To him, junk is much more interesting.

DeShawn loves his autism. He thinks it makes him smart in science. He wants to be an inventor when he grows up. Plus, the neighborhood kids think that the stuff DeShawn builds is really cool.

Chances are, you feel more comfortable when things in your life are the same: your clothes, the food you eat, the activities you do. If things change, you might get upset. Even so-called simple things, like wearing a different kind of pants or getting a new bedspread, might make you nervous. You probably like routines so life is easier to predict.

Talia's Story

Talia is a fifth grader with ASD, but she never really knew she had a "problem" until this year. At school, she has to go to the social skills room to meet with the social worker and three other students. They talk about how to make friends. But Talia doesn't think she needs to make friends. After all, she's friendly with everyone. Sometimes people think she's *too* friendly.

She'll talk about her favorite things with anyone who listens. And she loves explaining about all her stuffed animals—their names, how they look, and the magical world she's created for them. Lately, some adults have been telling Talia that other kids her age aren't that interested in stuffed animals anymore. These adults want Talia to learn to talk about other things. Talia wonders, "How could anyone *not* be interested in stuffed animals?"

At night when Talia goes to bed, she takes all of her stuffed animals and organizes them on her bookshelf. They each have to be in the exact right spot in order for Talia to feel happy and ready to sleep. One night she couldn't find Lennon, her stuffed turtle, and that meant she couldn't go to sleep. Talia's mom and dad got frustrated. Her parents love her. But they don't love her ASD because it makes her get "stuck" on things.

Now Talia wonders what all the fuss is about. Is she really so different? Are people always going to be frustrated with her? Does being friends *have* to be hard? Talia knows she has lots to think about. In some ways, she's glad she can go to the social worker to ask all the questions that are on her mind. Talia's parents say they'll always be there to talk with too.

Sometimes, people with ASD have repetitive behaviors that calm or soothe them. Maybe they rock back and forth, pace, spin in a circle, hum, or flick their hands. Maybe you have habits like these that you hardly notice, just like some people bite their fingernails when they're nervous or fiddle with a pen when they're bored. It may even come as a surprise to you when other people point out what you're doing and ask you to stop. (By the way, these movements are called *stims,* and you can read more about them in Chapter 17.)

A Word About "Differences"

It can be a real challenge to have ASD. There are differences in how you communicate, socialize, and behave. This doesn't mean you *can't* communicate, make friends, or get along at home. You just have your own unique style in these areas.

When you read the stories about Talia and DeShawn, did you notice that other people sometimes were frustrated about these kids' behaviors and challenges? Family members and friends don't always understand what it means to have autism spectrum disorder. There are things these people need to learn too!

You can help the people in your life by saying:

"Having ASD means I act differently sometimes."

"Everyone has challenges—this is one of mine."

"I'm doing the best I can."

"Sometimes I need extra help."

"I'm just being myself!"

Or:

"I have ASD, but I can still learn and grow. And this means you can too."

Chapter 3

ASD and the Senses

Chapter 2 explained the three main symptoms of ASD: difficulties with communication, social skills, or behavior. Lots of people with ASD also have differences in how their senses (like hearing and taste) do their jobs.* These differences, called *sensory issues,* are another symptom of ASD.

As soon as you arrived in the world, your senses began to shape your experiences. It's through the senses that you learn to understand yourself, other people, and your environment. When your senses work differently, the way you experience the world is very unique.

This has its ups and downs. On the upside, you have *intensity.* When you love something, you really, *really* love it. You might have laser-like focus. You probably notice details that no one else in your family or classroom is aware of. Autism spectrum disorder is a special way of perceiving the world and living in it. This way may not be typical, but it's *yours.*

On the downside, the world is often noisy, bright, busy, messy, social, and full of chaos. All kinds of input is coming at you: voices, movement, faces, textures, sounds. That's a lot to take in, especially if your processing speed is slower or your senses are different from many people's.

How Some People with ASD Explain It

Temple Grandin is a famous doctor of animal science, a professor, and an author. She also has autism. Successful today, she faced many challenges growing up with ASD. Thanks to her books and lectures, the world understands more about the experience of autism and how it may affect someone's life.

*The chart on page 29 describes the senses.

Temple says she was overwhelmed by her senses as a child. Loud noises were terribly painful to her ears. Her underwear felt like sandpaper against her skin. She would flinch if the teacher touched her. She says that being hugged by her affectionate aunt was "like being suffocated by a mountain of marshmallows."

So Temple spent her days dreaming up comfort machines in her mind. One idea was a suit that inflated like a plastic beach toy. The suit would apply comforting pressure to her body. Another idea was to build a special heated enclosure "about three feet wide and three feet tall—just big enough so I could get into it and close the door." There she'd feel safe and secure.

Do you sometimes get overwhelmed by all that's going on around you—the sights, smells, and sounds? Maybe you sometimes long for a dark, quiet place where you can be away from the world and feel peaceful.

Or maybe you have the opposite problem: You need *more* input from your eyes, ears, and body to get your senses working better. This is another common experience for people with ASD.

Donna Williams, an artist and a writer with autism, has said her sensory experience is "like having a brain without a sieve." *Sieves* are tools with tiny holes for straining liquids or collecting the finest bits of sand. You could say that a sieve *sorts* the liquids and solids that are poured into it. When your brain has trouble sorting information, the world can be a very confusing place with lots of distractions.

For example, when you're sitting in a classroom trying to listen to your teacher, it's easy to get distracted by:

- bright fluorescent lights that "hum"
- other students moving, talking, or whispering
- noises from the hallway or the ticking clock
- what your teacher *says* versus what he *writes* on the board
- how hard your chair is, or how close your desk is to another student's

With all that going on, no wonder it's challenging to pay attention to the lesson!

Then there's what's happening inside you. Hungry stomach? Nervousness? Sore fingers from writing? A sickening feeling because of the weird smells drifting from the cafeteria? Distracting!

And what about what's going on in your *brain*? (Another inside part.)

At times, your brain might unexpectedly get locked onto one of your special interests or fascinations. Suddenly you're thinking about your favorite video game . . .

or model cars

or card collection

or princess movies

or weather patterns

Luke Jackson, a young author who's written about his ASD, says his obsessions creep up on him like a thief in the night. "One minute I am just very interested in a topic and the next it seems as if my mind has been infiltrated by an army that stamps around and eradicates [erases] my everyday thoughts, replacing them with thoughts of computers."

Does that ever happen to you? Throughout the day, your brain might leap to thoughts about your favorite subject. This may be in response to "sensory overload"—or that feeling of being overwhelmed by what's going on both inside and outside of you. Is it "bad" that your brain and body may get distracted in unexpected ways? No. It's just part of ASD and a unique part of who you are.

When you have ASD, you need to find ways to help your senses work better for you. Take Temple Grandin as an example. As a young woman, she spent time working on a cattle ranch. There she watched as nervous, twitchy calves were put into a device called a "squeeze chute," which provided gentle pressure. The chute calmed them down. She became a bit obsessed with that device!

So, what did she do? She built a squeeze machine for *herself.* Inside this device, she felt calmer. She could control the amount of pressure on her body and relax. This was just one step on her long journey to understanding herself and her autism.

For Donna Williams, art became a way of expressing her sensory experience of color, texture, and pattern. She calls her work "ARTism." Maybe you too can find new ways of expressing yourself through paint and clay.

Both of these women grew up during a time when not much was known about ASD. But now, lots of experts are paying attention to the sensory needs of people with autism. This means you don't have to figure out on your own what might help you feel better. That's good news.

You might want to take a close look at the chart on page 29 and think about your own senses. Are some of the sensory issues listed familiar to you? Are there other ones that you've experienced? Write them down if you'd like. The list you create can help the adults in your life figure out whether certain types of therapy and activities might help you.

Making Sense of the Senses

This chart shows seven senses that can play a role in how you feel:

Sense	Where it comes through	What happens
Sight	Eyes	Light may be too bright and disturbing. Or you might have difficulty "tracking" moving objects with your eyes.
Hearing	Ears	Loud noises may be painful, or you may not be able to tune out background noises. Maybe you react strongly to sharp, high-pitched sounds.
Smell	Nose	Some smells might make you gag or feel sick. Or you may tend to sniff objects to get information to your brain.
Taste	Mouth	You might love some tastes (like salty) but hate others, and avoid certain food textures (like crunchy or mushy). Or, you might enjoy licking objects to discover their taste and the sensation in your mouth.
Touch	Skin	Certain fabrics might feel unusually itchy or scratchy to you. Sometimes a light touch feels like a push. Maybe you resist touch—or perhaps you crave it. You might enjoy the pressure of tight clothing and tight hugs.
Balance (also called *vestibular*)	Inner ear	You might have difficulty balancing, riding a two-wheeler, walking on uneven surfaces, or using stairs. Maybe you feel stressed out when your feet leave the ground. You may hate or love spinning.
Body awareness (also called *proprioception*)	Muscles and joints	It might be hard for you to understand where your body is in space. Do you tend to bump into people or objects? Or do you like to flop onto soft furniture and snuggle under heavy blankets? Coordinating your body's movements can be difficult. So can figuring out the steps you need to do for certain tasks.

> I have 'artillery'! Earplugs are a must—when I'm walking around, when I'm in the shop, when I'm in the car . . . I always have sunglasses and gloves for touch issues.
>
> —**Rudy Simone, author of** *Aspergirls: Empowering Females with Asperger's Syndrome*

Want a fun way to keep your senses engaged? Or to take your mind off something that's stressing you out? Ask a parent to stock up on sensory items. There are all sorts of stress balls you can squeeze or bounce. You can also try colorful items like pinwheels, balloons, yo-yos, or even a lava lamp. Get some whistles or a harmonica. Chew sugarless bubblegum. Make or buy some Play-Doh to squish and squash. Buy lots of bubble stuff to blow and pop. Or how about a mini trampoline to bounce on? Everyday items like these help keep your mouth, body, eyes, ears, and hands busy.

Chapter 4

Well-Known People with ASD

For many years, very little was known about autism. Today, all sorts of books, magazines, and websites talk about the condition. It's common to hear about ASD on the news and TV talk shows. Television programs now feature characters with ASD too.

Some people have been looking back in history to imagine whether anybody famous had autism. For example, researchers at Cambridge and Oxford Universities in England say that two of the world's most famous scientists may have had ASD:

Brilliant **Albert Einstein** developed the theory of relativity. But as a child, he was a loner. He had an obsessive way of repeating sentences until he was seven years old. Is this proof of ASD? Maybe.

Sir Isaac Newton discovered the laws of gravity (when an apple fell on his head, according to a long-standing story). He often got so interested in his work, he'd forget to eat. He had few friends and had a hard time socializing with them. Is this evidence of autism, or simply high intelligence?

Some people suggest that the musician and composer **Wolfgang Amadeus Mozart**, who was a musical genius, had traits of autism. Others think the talented artist **Andy Warhol**, known for his famous paintings of Campbell's soup cans, had signs of ASD. Because these men are no longer alive, it's impossible know the truth.

Autism and Talent

When it's said that famous people in history may have had autism, good and bad things happen. What's good is that people start talking about ASD. They take notice. They get curious. They realize ASD is a big part of many people's lives. Also, as a person with ASD, you realize that some of the most talented people on Earth may have had it too. That can inspire you.

What's *not* so good about all that talk of geniuses and autism? It leads people to think this: ASD = Genius. People might find out you have ASD and then expect you to be a "walking calculator." Or to have the ability to put 1,000-piece puzzles together as easy as one, two, three. The truth is, being a genius is uncommon for anyone, whether the person has ASD or not. It's also unusual to have an extraordinary talent that leads to fame and fortune.

Maybe you've heard of the movie *Rain Man* from 1988, about a man who was a genius in counting but couldn't take care of himself. The story was based on a real-life man named Kim Peek. Kim actually was born with damage to his brain, but he also had unique and incredible memorization skills. This condition made him seem like an "autistic savant." Because of the popularity of the movie, some people still think of *Rain Man* whenever they hear the word *autism*. But being a savant is really rare, whether someone has autism or not.

Another famous savant is Stephen Wiltshire, an artist with autism. He's been nicknamed "The Human Camera" because he can study a building for several minutes and then go to his desk and draw it from memory. Once, he flew over an area of London in a helicopter. Afterward he drew what he saw. He created a perfectly scaled drawing of a four-square-mile area of the city with 12 historic landmarks and 200 other structures. Now that's amazing!

Many people love stories like this. We enjoy discovering the potential of the human mind and finding unlikely heroes. Yet, most people with autism *don't* have a special talent. Maybe you do, and maybe you don't.

Like anyone else, you have a set of strengths and weaknesses. For example, you might do well in certain subjects in school and not so well in others. You could be into sports or music or theater, just like anybody. You might be good at "regular stuff" like collecting trading cards or reading comic books, like many people your age.

On the other hand, you might have a fascination or special hobby that someday leads to a talent or even a career.

Remember reading about Temple Grandin in Chapter 3? (See pages 25–26.) All her life she was interested in constructing things, in her mind and with her hands. She also had a special bond with animals. She somehow understood them more deeply than others could. Her job now combines both of those interests. Today, she is Dr. Temple Grandin, known for designing more humane ways to handle livestock (like cattle and pigs) at meat-processing plants.

Talent helped her—but *hard work* was a huge part of her success. So was persistence—that "stick-to-it" quality that anyone can learn. To find out more about Temple's life and challenges, you might want to check out the 2010 movie *Temple Grandin.*

Hard work also helped Stephen Wiltshire be successful (though his talents played a role too). He's been drawing steadily since he was seven years old. His work is part of who he is, like his autism.

You know another person who is talented and hardworking? Tom Angleberger. Maybe you've heard of him, or at least his books. He started with *The Strange Case of Origami Yoda*, a story about an oddball sixth grader called Dwight. Dwight folded an origami finger puppet of Yoda from *Star Wars.* Amazingly, that finger puppet seemed to have the ability to make predictions and give advice. The book was so popular, it led to follow-ups about Darth Paper, Fortune Wookie, and other *Star Wars*–based paper creations.

Tom not only writes for middle schoolers but also talks to groups of kids about his unique combination of disability and ability. He uses the term Asperger's (for more on that, see page 2) and refers to himself as an Aspie. He calls his Asperger's his "superpower."*

Tom has challenges with his communication, social skills, and interests. Writing in *The Guardian*, he suggests he can't eat without making a mess and can't look people in the eye. School was a real struggle for Tom. Here are his words:

> Running my mouth + bad social skills = awkward situations
>
> Awkward situations + bad social skills = humiliations, meltdowns, or both

Part of the problem was that words flooded his brain all the time. They overflowed out of his mouth. The constant flow of words was overwhelming to him.

But then—a discovery. If he typed the words into the computer, he could write stories! The middle-school kids in his books often deal with social situations gone wrong. They also have what Tom calls "TRIUMPHANT VICTORIES."

That word-flow problem? He turned it around, making it into a perk. A *job*. A way to connect with kids around the world.

Perhaps you see a theme here. Some people with disabilities find an ability to explore. So they work *with* it—and work *on* it. The ability doesn't magically arrive and lead to **SUCCESS.** It takes years of trying, learning, and growing.

*Read more about that on page 37.

Young People with ASD Today

Who are "young people"? This section of the book takes a look at a few well-known people in their teens and twenties. We (the authors) consider that young. These young people have been open—even outspoken—about their ASD. The focus here isn't on their fame but on how they shine a light on ASD.

If you watch the TV show *America's Got Talent*, you may know of the Season 14 winner Kodi Lee (who was age 22 at the time). Kodi is a singer and pianist. He is blind and has ASD. The judges recognized his talents right away. They gave him the "golden buzzer" that allowed him to go straight through to the live shows on the program. Kodi excels in jazz, rock, pop, classical, and R&B. His website explains that he has perfect pitch. That is the rare ability to sing or play a musical note without hearing it first. Kodi uses music to connect with others and to share what it means to have ASD.

Another talented musician with ASD is James Durbin. At age 22 he was a Top 4 contestant on the TV show *American Idol*, Season 10. During his time on *Idol*, James talked about how he has Asperger's syndrome (see page 2) and Tourette syndrome. (Tourette leads to his facial tics, or muscle movements he can't control.) He was teased and bullied as a child and teen. Music, he says, is what saved him. He joined the theater and performed in musicals. Being on stage raised his confidence. A huge fan of rock and roll, James has gone on to make several heavy-metal albums.

James explains that his ASD causes challenges. He doesn't like the feeling of washing his hair, for example. He often speaks without thinking first, which leads to social awkwardness. He gets stressed remembering the years of bullying he dealt with. But in the moments when he's performing, his tics seem to go away. He almost forgets about ASD. It's just him, the songs, and the fans.

Another famous person with ASD is Greta Thunberg. She's a student and an environmental activist. She rose to fame by speaking out, leading student protests, and launching strikes about the climate crisis. Greta was born in Stockholm, Sweden, and became a world traveler—an ocean-goer, in fact! In summer 2019, at age 16, Greta sailed across the Atlantic from England to New York in the 60-foot racing yacht called *Malizia II*. She wanted to cross the ocean without flying (because air travel harms the environment more). The voyage lasted 15 days. She then spoke at the United Nations Climate Action Summit, where she did *not* hold back.

She told political leaders and all the adults in the room: "You are failing us." She warned about environmental damage and the toll it will take on human beings. "People are dying. Entire ecosystems are collapsing," she said. "The eyes of all future generations are upon you." Many people were shocked. Many others cheered her frank and fiery speech. Since then, Greta has joined more climate protests. She talks to young people everywhere—adults too—about how to take better care of our planet. She was named *Time* magazine's 2019 Person of the Year.

And that's just a short list of Greta's accomplishments. If you want to know more about her, check out a biography or her own writings. You may even be inspired to learn more about climate change and youth activism.

If you research Greta Thunberg, you'll find that she has a few diagnoses: Asperger's syndrome, obsessive compulsive disorder (OCD), and selective mutism. In her own words, *selective mutism* "basically means I only speak when I think it's necessary. Now is one of those moments." When she was eight and first learning about the climate crisis, she didn't have any energy or friends. She developed eating problems. She became depressed. Life changed for Greta when she focused on raising people's awareness about climate change.

She knows she's different from most teens—way more intense, for instance. But the differences help her speak out. Like Tom Angleberger (page 33), Greta has even called her ASD her "superpower."

Huh? What's all this superpower talk? Is someone wearing a cape?

Having ASD doesn't give you magical abilities or superhuman strength. (Sorry, no time- travel talents or "spidey senses.") But this talk about superpowers can be a way to focus on positives instead of negatives. A way to see where you shine.

These young people with ASD have been in the spotlight. That means their stories and voices are being heard. They're part of the autism community, like you are. Each day, that community gets a little bigger and a lot stronger.

Your voice—your words and thoughts—are important too. Write down these thoughts in your journal or on a piece of paper, if you'd like. Here are some ideas to get you started:

Now that I know I have ASD, I feel . . .

My "ASD Heroes" could be . . .

The activity that I really love is . . .

When I do this activity, I feel . . .

Chapter 5

The "Big" Questions

Learning you have ASD isn't something that happens all at once. It takes time to understand what the diagnosis means. You may be thinking about yourself and your life differently than you did before. Most likely, you have questions that need answering.

This chapter gives you a Q&A (Question and Answer) of some of the hardest ASD questions. It doesn't have all the answers, but it's a starting point. If you have other questions, write them down. You can go to a parent, a teacher, or another trusted adult for answers.

Why Do Some People Have Autism?

(That's the million-dollar question!)

ANSWER: Doctors want to know what causes autism. So do families affected by ASD. Researchers are trying to find out. But, as of now, the answers just aren't clear. Experts *do* know that autism is partly genetic—meaning it starts in the *genes.*

What are genes? Every living organism has genes, which are like a set of instructions telling what the life form is like, how it survives, and how it behaves in its environment. Humans have thousands of genes. Think of genes as the computer program that makes each one of us what we are.

A number of genes play a role in autism. Some of these genes make a child more likely to have ASD. Other genes affect how a baby's brain develops. Still other genes determine how the brain cells communicate with each other.

Genes also play a part in how severe someone's symptoms of ASD may be. Some of these genes might be passed down from the parents. But other gene problems happen spontaneously (all of a sudden on their own).

How did experts find out that autism is partly genetic? They studied twins.

Researchers learned this: In identical twins, if one twin has autism there is a very good chance that the other will have it as well. However, if the twins are not identical (called *fraternal*), the chance is less than 10 percent that both twins will develop autism. Why this difference? Identical twins share more genes in common—that's what makes them identical! So the more genes the twins share in common, the more likely it is that they'll both have autism.

Environment plays an important role too. (We know this from the twins study as well.) Researchers want to know: Does a virus trigger autism? Are air pollutants involved? What about toxins in our environment? Just what is the cause of autism?

Most experts believe that ASD develops from a combination of factors. First, you must inherit some "genetic risk" from your parents. Then, something from your environment adds to that risk. However, experts don't know how much risk you must inherit. Or what the triggers in the environment may be.

The focus here is on *you* and questions you might have about ASD. Right now, the world of science doesn't yet understand what causes autism. Maybe by the time you're grown up, more will be known. New research is being done every day.

Why Me?

ANSWER: It's not easy to hear about your diagnosis and learn that your ASD will have a big effect on your life. One of the first questions that might come to mind is: "Why me? Why do *I* have to have ASD when other people don't?"

It's a good question, but there's no simple answer. Nobody gets to choose their genes. If we *could* choose them, we'd probably all choose to be incredibly intelligent, good-looking, athletic, and talented. We'd pick never having any kind of problem in life. If only that could happen . . .

But the reality is we all have a genetic code that determines how we look and grow. Think of all the characteristics that make you you. Your eye color, skin color, and hair color, for example, are a basic part of you. They were determined before you were born. Your height is already set in your genes, even though you aren't done growing yet. In the same way, certain things about your brain were preset as part of your genetic code. It's just what makes you who you are.

Will I Always Have Autism?

ANSWER: The short answer is yes—but there's more to it than that.

Sometimes people get an illness like a cold or virus, and it goes away after a few days or weeks. The symptoms lessen over time and eventually disappear. When you have a cold, you probably lie in bed, get lots of extra sleep, and drink liquids. Once your body has had enough time to fight the germ or virus, you get out of bed and back to your life.

Other illnesses are more serious and need medical attention. For example, you might have had strep throat before. Your doctor probably tested you for strep and then gave you an *antibiotic*—a medication that helps fight infection. In this case, the "cure" is an infection-fighting medication and lots of rest.

Then there are medical conditions that require ongoing treatment, like asthma. This lung condition causes coughing, wheezing, and difficult breathing. Maybe you know kids with asthma or have it yourself. Usually, the treatment includes breathing medications, such as an inhaler or pills. Having asthma means making some adjustments in life. For example, the person may get sick more often and need to see a doctor more frequently than other people do. But people with asthma still lead normal lives.

Autism spectrum disorder is different from the various types of illnesses and conditions just described. Why? For one thing, your body doesn't fight your ASD like an infection. For another thing, autism doesn't concern only a single part of the body (like the lungs). Autism affects your brain, body, and development.

Remember that part about genes on page 39? You are born with your autism, and it stays with you for life. Your symptoms aren't necessarily a sign of something that needs to be "cured." They're a part of you, just like your autism.

However, your symptoms may change as you change, learn, and grow. Many people with ASD leave some of their old behaviors behind. For instance, they may "flap" a lot as kids, but then do it less when they're older. They may learn to try new foods, instead of sticking with the same ones every day. They may find ways to become better sleepers or to make more friends. The changes don't happen automatically—they take some effort.

Just know this: As you grow and change, so will your ASD!

> [My] autism has gotten way better over the years. Only some parts aren't as good. When I feel upset, I feel as though I don't want to have autism anymore. When I do talented things like [my] art, it makes me feel as though autism is a good thing in some ways.
>
> —Max LaZebnik, from his article "A Journey Through Autism" in *The Autism Perspective (TAP)* Magazine

Long ago, doctors used to think of autism as a lifelong disability, one that made the person unable to learn or change. Back then, doctors had some low expectations for people with autism. But now with so many parents, educators, and experts trying to understand ASD and help kids, the view of autism is changing for the better. Now experts understand that the earlier in life you get your diagnosis, the sooner your ASD treatment can start. *Early intervention* is the key to a better life and future.

Still, many ASD experts are careful about using the term *cure.* They don't want to suggest that autism is curable because it's not a disease or an illness. Some people are more comfortable with the word *recover.* They say that a person can recover from some of the most challenging symptoms and feel better.

Other people, many of whom have ASD, don't like all this talk about cures and recovery. They want the world to know that autism isn't something negative. They don't like being thought of as "broken" or "in need of fixing." They're proud to be different, proud of who they are. They work to let people know that having ASD isn't about being a misfit, a genius, or someone to pity.

You are Someone with ASD—an individual. This means you have the right to think about autism in **your own unique way,** whatever that way may be.

> Don't feel sorry for me. I have autism, but I'm cool with who I am. I love lots of things about my life. . . . I will always have autism, but that doesn't mean my future won't be great.
>
> —Daniel Stefanski, from his book *How to Talk to an Autistic Kid*

Chapter 6

Think About It, Talk About It

Right now, you might feel confused about your ASD and what it means for your future. It's okay to feel that way. Give it time. Your feelings will change as you learn more about yourself and living with ASD.

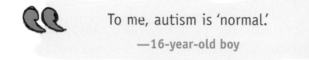

> To me, autism is 'normal.'
>
> —16-year-old boy

Everybody has personal stuff they need to work on. Everyone has things to celebrate about themselves too. In that way, we're all alike.

This chapter is about taking time to think and talk about what you've learned so far.

43

> ## *Note for Adults*
> The Introduction for Adults (page 5) and Sharing the Diagnosis with Your Child (page 235) contain information that may be helpful as you talk with a child about questions, worries, feelings, and coping strategies.

Ask questions. It's likely you have lots of questions about your ASD and how it will affect your life. Who can you ask? Make a list of your helpers: a parent, your doctor, a therapist or counselor, a social worker, a teacher, a school counselor, and other adults you trust. (Chapter 7 is all about helpers.) Maybe your dad or mom can find a support group for kids and families affected by ASD. A group like this can be a great place to share questions and learn more.

Talk about your feelings. You probably have mixed feelings about all you're learning about ASD. Talking about feelings can help. You can go to a parent or relative, an older sibling, or another adult you trust. These people may not have all the answers, but they can listen. And they might be able to find other people who can support you.

Draw or write about your feelings. Everyone has strong emotions that need to be expressed. Why not keep a feelings journal? Journals come in all shapes and sizes. There are big ones with fancy covers, little diaries with a lock and key, or plain old spiral-bound notebooks. You can also keep a journal on a computer at home, if you prefer.

Journals are for your own private words, so write anything you want. Don't worry about whether the handwriting looks sloppy or whether your punctuation is correct. You can also sketch in your journal, paint in it, draw comic strips, or make collages.

Express your feelings in healthy ways. Many people with ASD have difficulty handling their feelings and managing strong emotions like anger, fear, and frustration. You might struggle to hold your temper or have frequent meltdowns when your days are rough. Over time, you can learn to handle those feelings more successfully. (See Chapter 16 for more on that.) Meanwhile, there are healthy ways to express strong feelings without hurting yourself or others. Try running around, swinging, dancing, or bouncing on a mini trampoline. You could scribble, pound a hunk of clay, or bang on a drum.

Get to know your ASD community. Your family can look for a social skills group for you. Or they can seek out other people with ASD in your town or city. See "Where to Go for More Info" on page 233 for a list of organizations that can help.

A Message for You

There's a commercial on TV and the internet where the people push a big red button to make everything easier. It's called the Easy Button. The idea is that you push it and—*poof!*—you get just what you need when you need it, and life is *goooood*.

Well, there's no Easy Button when it comes to ASD. But some things do get easier.

Over time, you'll learn ways to manage your symptoms and handle your feelings. Your body will get stronger, and you'll most likely become better able to do things that seem hard right now. With practice, communication can get easier and so can being social. You'll find friends, and these buddies will help make life more fun.

You have some challenges ahead, but you've got what it takes to meet them. Instead of an Easy Button, how about an "I Can Do It!" Button?

Kayla's Story

Kayla is quirky—at least that's what her mom always tells her. Her mom says that quirky means "special and unique, like no one else." Kayla already knows that every person is special and different from everyone else, so she doesn't spend much time thinking about being quirky. But now that she's in sixth grade, Kayla is starting to look back. Maybe there's more to being special and unique than she realized.

When Kayla was 3 years old, her family sometimes called her "Quiet One." Although she could speak very well, she rarely said a word when she was at preschool or in a group. The preschool teacher told Kayla's mom, "Don't worry, Kayla is just shy." In kindergarten, Kayla had trouble in the mornings. She never wanted to wear a dress or loose pants, only leggings. She was always sad when her mom dropped her off for the day, and sometimes Kayla cried. The kindergarten teacher said Kayla was a little anxious.

In third grade, the lunch servers said Kayla was a picky eater because she always chose exactly the same foods in the cafeteria each day. And in fifth grade, some of the other girls made fun of Kayla because she preferred to climb the climbing wall at recess rather than talk with them. Kayla wished she could climb all day long. She loved the firm, chunky feeling of the hand-holds and felt a thrill each time she reached the top of the wall. And she felt so much calmer after a few minutes of climbing. Because of what other people said about her, Kayla started to think of herself as a quiet, shy, picky-eater climber.

Kayla is a good student, and her best class is spelling. The other kids in school often come up to her and ask her to spell words. It almost feels like they think she's a trained animal in the circus performing tricks. The kids try to stump her by giving her hard words to spell, but Kayla has no trouble! Spelling just comes easily to her.

Kayla likes being smart, and she loves learning at school. But she often feels lonely. Other kids talk to her—but they don't invite her over or ask her to come to their birthday parties. Kayla has some friends, but not as many as other people do. When she tells her mom about her worries, her mom usually says, "Don't worry, Kayla, you're just a little quirky."

As a sixth grader, Kayla has an important job at school: being a helper for the first graders learning to spell. It's fun, but when the social worker at school first told Kayla about the special job, he mentioned it would help Kayla build her social skills. "What?" she thought. "Why do I need to learn social skills?" She knew she needed to talk to her mom to get some answers.

Kayla got up the courage to ask her mom an important question: "*Why* am I quirky?"

They talked for a long time. Kayla's mom told her she has autism, which affects her ability to be social. The autism, Mom explained, is a part of Kayla, but it's not all she is.

Kayla started to understand why she preferred the same foods every day, and why she only felt comfortable in certain clothes. It was almost a relief to finally understand more about herself. She had lots of questions over the next few days, and her mom did her best to answer them. Kayla and her mom went to the bookstore to get a book about autism so Kayla could read more about it.

Now Kayla has a deeper understanding about the things that made her different when she was younger—things that continue to make her unique. This doesn't mean she understands everything about herself or about autism, but that's okay. Kayla now knows she isn't just a quiet, shy, picky-eater tomboy who can spell really well.

Tonight, as her mom sits with her before bedtime, Kayla says: "Autism—I can spell that, Mom. Q-U-I-R-K-Y. Goodnight!"

Chapter 7

Your Team of Helpers

During the process of getting a diagnosis for ASD and being treated, you'll probably meet lots of different experts. Think of these people as your personal helpers. Autism spectrum disorder is a condition that affects the brain and body. Because of this, you might need to see experts who have knowledge of both. This chapter tells you "Who's Who."

Neurologist: A neurologist is a doctor who studies the brain and brain disorders. This doctor may see you to decide if you need special tests of your brain—such as an EEG to measure brain waves, or an MRI or CT scan of your head to take pictures of your brain. Some people with ASD have other medical problems such as seizures. A neurologist helps treat those issues.

Pediatrician: Pediatricians are doctors who take care of children and teens. A pediatrician can provide checkups and give you medications when you're sick with an infection or a virus. You've probably been seeing a pediatrician since you were a baby. This doctor may have been the first to notice your signs of autism and send you to a **developmental pediatrician** for further tests.

Psychiatrist: Psychiatrists are doctors who help with behavior and emotional problems. They do this by teaching you and your family new ways to manage and cope. Psychiatrists may also prescribe medications to help with difficulties such as attention span, moodiness, sleep problems, hard-to-handle feelings, or meltdowns.

Psychologist: A psychologist works with people to understand emotional issues and solve problems. A psychologist may give you special tests to help understand your learning levels. (This can help you do better at school.) Psychologists also help families learn to handle living with autism. Or, a psychologist may help with communication and social skills.

Occupational therapist (OT): OTs do tests to check your body coordination compared to other people your age. Based on the results, the OT comes up with a plan to help you develop more strength and coordination. Occupational therapists may also look at how you react to light, sound, taste, smell, and touch so you can get help with sensory issues. (See Chapter 3 for more on that.) You may go to an OT if you need help with daily activities like buttoning, tying shoes, or writing.

Physical therapist (PT): PTs are experts in muscle strength and development. They can measure the range of motion in your joints. They can help you with mobility (how you move). And they can show you exercises that may improve the way your body works. When you have physical therapy, you might work on riding a bike or gaining more strength and balance.

 My advice is . . . to follow the advice
your parents and doctors give you.

—14-year-old boy

Speech therapist: A speech therapist helps with communication—mainly, your ability to speak and use language. People with ASD almost always need to see a speech therapist because communication problems are a main symptom. At speech therapy, you may learn to pronounce words more clearly or practice conversation skills. Or you might learn to use a special communication system instead of words.

Special education teacher: This is an expert at your school who observes how you learn and interact with others. A special ed teacher notes whether you can pay attention in class and how well you learn reading, math, and other subjects. This teacher also notices how you get along with other kids your age. Special ed teachers are trained to spot behavior issues and help kids learn new ways to manage.

The list of experts doesn't stop there. Other helpers may include a **behavioral therapist** who can help you improve how you behave at home with your family. Or, you might visit with a **nutritionist** to get information on eating healthy foods or taking vitamins. At school, you might see the **social worker, school counselor,** or **reading specialist.** You may also have a **classroom aide** or **paraprofessional.**

Some kids with autism even get a service dog. These dogs are specially trained to help a child stay calmer at home and in public places, for example. Many families have found that having a dog helps a child with ASD feel more comfortable in social situations too.

[My dog] Henry was just really gentle, friendly, and sociable. I liked that he had a wise look on his face and I always trusted him, which made me feel very comfortable with him. . . . It made me feel good when people admired him and would talk to me about him.

—Dale, a boy with autism, from the book *A Friend Like Henry: The Remarkable Story of an Autistic Boy and the Dog That Unlocked His World*

After reading this chapter about getting a team of helpers, you may think "Well, that's a *lot* of helpers for just one person!" True. And if you have this many helpers, it means you also have a lot of new faces and places to deal with. Autism spectrum disorder is complicated. Whether you have a few helpers or a lot, each one is an expert in certain areas of autism. Together, this team of helpers can advise you, teach you new skills, and make sure you stay healthy.

This book can be a part of *your* team. If you'd like, you can come up with a team name. A strong team:

- listens
- shares information
- adjusts to change
- keeps trying, even when the going gets tough!

You are the heart of this team. The things you do to help yourself will make life with ASD easier for you.

Although your team may be full of experts, they will probably tell you this: You and your family are truly the experts when it comes to YOU. None of the experts live with you around the clock. They can't observe your every strength and challenge. That's why it's so important for you and your family to learn what works well for you and what you might need to change. Then you can go to your helpers with lots of information, ideas, and questions (not just once but at each new appointment).

Over time, as you learn more about your ASD and yourself, you'll become your own expert—with a little help from your family and team.

Home, School, Community

Chapter 8

Family Matters

Have you heard of a safe harbor? A safe harbor is a place boats set out from and return to after going to sea. The waters in the harbor are calm, and the boats are protected from the wind and waves. A family is a kind of safe harbor too. It's the place we leave and come home to. It's where we can feel comfortable and safe. In the best of worlds, families provide not only shelter but also love, support, and acceptance. Home needs to be a place where people understand your quirks and differences, and love you no matter what.

Maybe your home fits this description. Maybe not. Not all homes do. Some aren't places where kids feel cared for and accepted. When this happens, other people can step in to help: grandparents, aunts, uncles, cousins, older siblings, other relatives, or family friends. Whoever takes care of you—whoever acts as your safe harbor—is *family* in the best sense of the word. They're the people who can help you figure out your ASD, your strengths, your challenges, and your path in life.

In this chapter, we talk about ways that families can support your social growth. You and the adults who read this *Survival Guide* with you will learn about four social skills that start at home:

1. using manners

2. playing fair

3. handling conflict

4. doing your share

These skills not only improve your communication, but also build your confidence. And there's an added benefit: They can help strengthen family bonds.

Skill #1: Using Manners

Manners are rules to help people understand how to behave in social settings. When you have manners, you have a better idea of how to act around others. That builds your confidence and improves your social skills. People notice when you're polite. They'll be more likely to see you as thoughtful and nice to be around.

There are a few important "manners words" you can use every day to improve your communication (see page 56). Practice them as much as you can with your family. The more you use these words at home, the more you'll use them away from home too.

You can go to freespirit.com/SGforASD to download the "Manners Words" list. Keep it someplace handy. The more you practice using manners words, the more they'll come to you automatically—without your having to think about what to say.

Manners Words

What to say	When to say it
"Hello" (or "Hi")	When you first see someone
"Good-bye" (or "Bye")	When you or someone else is leaving
"Please"	When you want something
"Thank you"	When someone gives you what you want
"You're welcome"	When someone says "Thank you"
"Excuse me"	Whenever you bump into someone, need to get by people, or have to interrupt someone who's talking
"Yes, please"	When you want something being offered to you
"No, thank you"	When you don't want what's being offered
"I'm sorry"	When you hurt someone or make a mistake

There is one thing you and your family can get to work on right away: using manners words—and other manners—at mealtime. Mealtime tends to be a stressful time for someone who has ASD—and that means it's stressful for the whole family. For example:

Mali hated dinnertime because she didn't like all the waiting: Waiting for everyone to get to the table. Waiting for food. Waiting for everyone to finish. In her opinion, dinner took way too much time. She'd rather eat by herself in a separate room, where it was quiet and she could go at her own pace (fast!). She knew it was polite to wait and to share mealtime with her family, but it was hard for her to do those things.

Zach knew that sitting at the table with his family meant conversation. His mom explained that talking together at mealtime was courteous. But it was hard for him to figure out what to say and when to say it. Sometimes his mom asked him not to interrupt so much, and his sister said he was too loud. Zach thought dinner was a big pain. He didn't like having to be a part of the conversation. Questions like "How was your day?" annoyed him. It was better on weekends when his family sometimes ate in front of the TV.

J.J. didn't like people watching him while he ate. They wanted him to be polite and use a fork and spoon, but J.J. liked to use his fingers. His parents told him to use his napkin, not his shirt, to wipe his hands. It seemed he was always making a mess somehow, by spilling or dropping stuff. Sometimes, food disgusted him, especially if it touched any other food on the plate.

It might seem as if everything goes wrong at mealtime. It's supposed to be a time for a family to gather, share a meal, and talk. But people sometimes end up forgetting their manners. They complain about the food, get into arguments, or stomp away from the table in a huff.

To make mealtime better, your family can set *positive* goals—goals that tell you what *to* do instead of what *not* to do. Here are examples of what other families have done:

Mali's parents used a visual timer to keep her at the dinner table longer. The first night, they only made her stay five minutes. But each night, they added one minute more. It wasn't long before Mali got used to staying at the table for as long as dinner lasted. The timer helped her see that it wasn't as hard to wait as she'd thought.

Zach's family turned dinnertime into "game time." It was easier for Zach to sit with his family if they talked about familiar things. One made-up game they played was "Animals That Start With." A family member picked a letter, and each player took turns naming a mammal, reptile, or fish that started with that letter. They did this until no one could think of another animal. Thinking ahead and wondering what people would say kept Zach at the table longer. In between turns, the family could work on other skills, such as manners for eating or trying new foods. Not every night was game night, though. On some nights they practiced polite conversation. That was okay with Zach because now dinnertime had become more enjoyable overall.

J.J.'s mom got him a special plate that had dividers on it, so each food could stay in its own section. She also took J.J. to a store to pick out his own utensils. He got a fork, knife, and spoon with a superhero theme. Then he found superhero napkins and a cup with a handle, which made it easier for him to hold (so he didn't spill as often). J.J. was excited to use these items at mealtime. It took some practice for him to get into the habit of using utensils and a napkin, but he did it! His dad promised him that after dinner each night, they'd do something special together: throw a ball, play with action figures, or work with tools. Having an after-dinner reward gave J.J. something to look forward to.

What could *your* mealtime goals be? Here are some ideas to pick from:

- I will try one new food.
- I will stay at the table until everyone is finished.
- I will ask each family member one question.
- I will talk about one thing that happened today.
- I will clear my plate.

> ### Note for Adults
>
> Mealtime goals can work for *every* child in the family, not just the one who has ASD. Often, the child with autism is singled out as the one who needs help—but all children benefit from working on manners and social skills.
>
> Also, you might want to try rewards for added motivation. They give kids something concrete to look forward to and work toward. Even simple rewards—stickers, quarters, or small toys—can be inspiring.

To stay on top of your goals, it helps to have a reminder you can see so you know how you're doing. A behavior chart is a simple tool that lets you track your progress each day. You can photocopy the one on page 60, or download a copy at freespirit.com/SGforASD. You can use the Behavior Chart for other behavior issues you want to work on too—not just for mealtime.

Make a fresh copy each week as you're working on your goals, and then fill in the chart every day. The chart includes space for up to three goals each week, but you can focus on only one or two goals if you'd like. Be sure to make your goals *positive*—write down what you *will* do, instead of what you need to stop doing. Fill in the boxes with a star, checkmark, point, or smiley face.

Skill #2: Playing Fair

Many kids who have ASD *love* games—video games, board games, in-the-car games, you name it! Games are fun, and there's another bonus—they're a social opportunity. Your family can use games to help you practice social skills, like taking turns and getting comfortable with letting others choose what *they* want to play. In turn, you can help them with their game-playing skills—because you're probably really good at remembering rules, facts, trivia, strategies, shortcuts, or whatever else comes up.

Behavior Chart

My behavior goals for the week of _____

Goal 1: _____

Sunday	Monday	Tuesday	Wednesday	Thursday	Friday	Saturday

Goal 2: _____

Sunday	Monday	Tuesday	Wednesday	Thursday	Friday	Saturday

Goal 3: _____

Sunday	Monday	Tuesday	Wednesday	Thursday	Friday	Saturday

How I will be rewarded: _____

_____   _____
Your signature   Parent/guardian signature

But here's a question for you: Do you sometimes get so caught up in a game that you almost forget about the other players? Maybe you ignore them when they ask to switch to another game or say they want to quit. Sometimes, you might even insist they keep playing because *you're* having so much fun. Remember, other kids usually aren't as intense as you are. You might be able to stay focused for hours on an activity you love, and you might really, *really* enjoy the repetition involved. But here's the problem: "Typical" kids often don't share that ability or level of interest. You might be able to play Monopoly or Mastermind all day, but after a while your friends and family probably get bored.

One of the best social skills you can learn through games is being a good sport. That doesn't mean you play sports, necessarily. Good *sportsmanship,* as it's called, is more about positive behaviors during games. It means you play by the rules—you play fair. You show that you're a good sport by treating the other players well. You can be a good sport whether you play for a team or prefer activities like Nintendo or board games.

Being a good sport may mean working on something that's a struggle for many kids on the spectrum: *knowing it's okay to lose.* People with ASD often have a need to win. They hate to be "wrong," or they feel very strongly that losing means they've "failed." For example, do you get upset if you're losing a game? Do the other players tell you to calm down or chill out? Do you sometimes insist other players must be cheating if you're behind in the game? If so, this probably happens because you feel a need to be right or "perfect."

It may give you a sense of relief to know that *nobody* is perfect, and *you* don't have to be either. The point of games is to have fun and get along with other people during play. Winning really isn't as important as it seems. You may be thinking, "Oh, *yes* it is." But if you want to be social and have fun playing games with other people, everyone's enjoyment is more important than who wins.

Changing your attitude about winning takes time—and some practice. Try this: When you lose a game, instead of getting upset, take a few deep breaths. Shake your arms and legs to get rid of nervous energy and bad feelings. Turn to the other players and say "Good game" or

"Nice job." Your words will help the others feel pleased and proud. *You* can feel proud too, because you're working on being a good sport. There's another payoff for you as well: People will want to play with you again if you're a good sport and don't get upset about losing. That means more game time!

Just for fun, your family can work with you to turn *losing* into a game. Next time you play something, do your *worst*. Make all the wrong moves—be silly and don't even try to win! You'll see that the game won't have as much intensity, and maybe you'll even laugh your way through it. Afterward, reward yourself with something that makes you feel good . . . extra time on your hobby, for example. This is a fun way for your family to support you on a skill that takes time to develop. You don't have to play this way all the time, of course! Just once in a while as a reminder that games can be silly, social, and even more surprising than they usually are.

6 Tips for Being a Good Sport with Family Members

1. Can't agree on a game? Take turns playing one you like and one your sister or brother likes. Flip a coin to see who picks first.

2. Take turns going first. Do this especially with activities that include longer turns (like video games).

3. If you win the game, don't brag about it or tease the other person about losing. Just say something like "Good game—maybe you'll win next time." If you lose the game, congratulate the other player on winning. People appreciate compliments—they like to know when they've done well.

4. If you're playing an athletic game, shake hands or give high fives after it's over to show good sportsmanship.

5. Don't cheat or make up rules—play by the game rules. Cheating isn't fair. (Plus, other people don't like playing with someone who cheats.)

6. Remember, the reason people play games is to *have fun*. So, have fun! Don't worry so much about winning. Do your best and learn from your mistakes. In games, *luck* plays a part in how things turn out. If you don't win, better luck next time.

Skill #3: Handling Conflict

Your family is your training ground for getting along with other people at school, in your community, and in the wider world. At home, you probably have your share of troubles: You may disagree with a rule your parents make. You might get in fights with siblings. Maybe you feel upset about something and take out those negative feelings on everyone else. All of this is a normal part of family life, whether you have ASD or not.

> I have a 9-year-old sister. We get along sometimes, and I like to play games with her. I don't like when she sings or gets loud, which is most of the time.
>
> —14-year-old boy

> I don't get along well with my younger brother. Sometimes we play video games together or swim, but he annoys me. I annoy him too.
>
> —12-year-old boy

But having ASD tends to make conflict more difficult. For one thing, you probably have strong emotions that you're still figuring out how to handle. (You can read more about that in Chapter 16.) For another thing, you may have sensory issues (see Chapter 3) that increase your feelings of discomfort and make it harder for you to learn self-control.

When a conflict comes up, you need a plan. This plan should be simple enough to remember and use—even in situations that upset you a lot. You know what's simple? A traffic light. Red for stop, yellow for caution, and green for go. Your plan can be as basic as STOP THINK GO.

As soon as an argument or conflict begins, and you feel yourself getting upset, STOP. Put on the brakes so you won't do something to make the situation worse.

THINK a moment before you do anything. Take a few deep, calming breaths. What's the best way to handle the situation? This isn't a time to get physical (hitting, punching) or to say something that will be hard to take back.

Next, GO ahead and act. Give your best response, based on the questions you've asked yourself. Be sure to choose an action that *helps*—one that won't get you into trouble or make things worse.

Imagine this happens to you: Your little brother grabs the game controller right out of your hands and starts pushing the buttons. He's totally messing up your game.

Here's how to use STOP THINK GO:

STOP. Put on those brakes—keep your hands, feet, and words to yourself. You might want to yell, but instead, try to stay as calm and cool as you can. If you start to cry, that's okay—it happens!

Pay attention to your body's signals: Do you feel hot, shaky, jumpy, or ready to burst?

These are your body's warning signs to STOP. If you have a temper and you're used to screaming and yelling, then stopping yourself is tough. But it's *really* important. Keep practicing, and over time you'll get better at it.

THINK. Consider what happened. Maybe your little brother just wants to get your attention. He might think he's being funny or that it's his turn. Ask yourself:

What do I need to do to stay calm? I can take deep breaths.

What can I do that will HELP the situation? I can keep my hands to myself. I can calmly tell my brother that I didn't like what he did.

How do I avoid doing something that might HURT me or somebody else? Instead of thinking about how mad I am, I can focus on staying calm. If my brother tries to apologize, I can listen.

GO. Walk away from your brother. Get an adult's help. If you're able to calmly explain what happened, the adult is more likely to listen and help you resolve the conflict.

STOP THINK GO is easy to remember and, over time, it becomes easier to use. But it takes practice. Some families practice together by role-playing. They act out different situations (such as conflicts about bedtime, getting dressed for school, or helping with chores). Role-playing like this helps kids understand what works well in conflict situations and what doesn't. Another option is to work with a therapist on conflict-resolution skills. You can read more about conflict and how to handle it in chapters 12 and 13.

Skill #4: Doing Your Share

Everyone in a family has jobs. Parents work outside the home or in the home. They make the food, do the laundry, and keep things clean. If no one did these tasks, your home would be a confusing place to live.

Just like adults, kids can do jobs too. You and your siblings probably have a few chores, like feeding the pets or keeping rooms clean. Lots of kids (whether they have ASD or not) don't like chores. But chores are a "have to." When they don't get done, your home is less organized and your parents won't be too pleased.

Like other kids, you probably don't enjoy chores. In your case it may go further: *maybe you really hate doing chores,* and it's hard for you to get them done. In some families, parents avoid giving any chores to their child who has ASD because it leads to tears and angry outbursts. Does that happen in your home? Do you cry and get upset if you have to make your bed, for example? Or do you put up a fight so everyone will just leave you alone?

Maybe you don't have any chores. Or maybe you usually get out of doing them. But if that's the case, then you're not learning the skills you need to grow up and become independent someday. Other kids are learning those skills—you need them too! You have ASD, but you can still do your share. That's part of family life.

Remember in chapters 1 and 2, when you learned that ASD is a brain difference? This difference may make it harder for you to stay organized and figure out the most efficient way to complete tasks. What does that mean? It could mean that you don't notice when your space is messy. Or that you don't remember you're supposed to clean up. Maybe you start a task but aren't sure what steps to take and in which order. Perhaps you get confused and frustrated, and you give up. What can you do?

Get an adult's help. If you're reading this book with a grown-up, you can talk together about why chores are challenging for you. Then, start small. With the adult's help, practice each step of a given chore, even the littlest steps! You can do this at home, or perhaps with an occupational therapist (OT).

Look at the top of the next page to see how someone might break down one chore into its smallest parts.

My chore: Feed the dog
When? 7 am and 6 pm EVERY DAY
How much food? 1½ cups per feeding

Step 1. Get out bag of dry food.
Step 2. Get measuring cup.
Step 3. Measure the correct amount.
Step 4. Pour it into the dog's dish.
Step 5. Check to see if dog has fresh water.
　　　　If not, refill water dish.
Step 6. Put away dog food and measuring cup.

I rock!

You'll probably need a chore chart to keep track of your tasks. This way, you can see what you need to do each day. You can check off each job after it's completed. You can ask your dad or mom if there can be a reward system for doing chores, like an allowance or special treats. You can also talk together about whether there are consequences for not getting a chore done.

The key here is *practice*! It's okay if you need to be shown—again and again—how to get a task done. It's all right to break down the chore into very small steps so you can get the hang of it. And it's fine to ask for help if you need it. This is all part of the learning process.

Most kids who have ASD need tools to help them each day. There are many tools to try, such as calendars, visual schedules, daily planners, to-do lists, alarm clocks or timers, chore charts, bulletin boards, sticker charts, and little rewards. Experiment to see what helps you. Use whatever works!

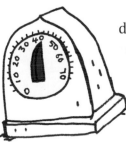

Chapter 9

Have Fun!

Sometimes, life with ASD means a lot of therapy, and doctor's appointments, and social skills practice . . . and the list goes on. This focus on your healthcare and communication is important, but life can't be *all* work. You're still a kid! That means you like to have fun, right? You need to play, just like other kids your age. Like anyone else, you've got to find time for physical activities, a hobby, music, art, a collection, crafts, a club, or volunteering—whatever you most enjoy. That's why this chapter is focused on FUN.

Play Is Good for You

So, here's the thing about having ASD: It can affect not only how you play, but also your level of imagination. Does this mean you don't know how to play? Or that you lack imagination? Hardly! You just have your own unique style when it comes to play. And the growth of your imagination may take more time. Unlike "typical" kids, you may gain skills at a different rate, or in an unusual order.

For example, maybe you started reading at a very young age, long before your peers knew their ABCs. Perhaps when you were little, you could do simple math problems or memorize all the capital cities in North America. While other kids were doing lots of play and pretend, you were focused on other types of activities.

Or perhaps you've struggled in academic subjects. Not every child who has ASD shows an early ability in math, reading, or memorization. Maybe you're working at a different pace than other kids your age. Your brain is developing in its own way, on its own schedule.

Because of your ASD, skills such as being playful and imaginative may come more slowly for you. But they'll come, and you can help them get there.

Use Your Imagination

When you use imagination, you're able to look at the world in a different way. You can picture things that aren't there. Or pretend you're someone—or some*thing*—else. Imagination helps you be creative. It also helps you learn to solve problems.

You have imagination that you can use every day. This may mean trying new things. If you tend to do the same type of play over and over (because you like the repetition and familiarity), it's harder for family and friends to join you. Try new games or new ways of playing old favorites. For instance, change some of the rules or add a touch of humor: Keep Away is extra fun when the ball is a water balloon. Hide and Seek is spookier in the dark with flashlights.

At home, with the help of an adult, you might make a list of play activities you think you'll like. Then, over a period of time, *do* them— preferably with other people your age. This could be as simple as playing chase, kickball, tag, or four square more often. Or you could get out the board games, cards, and puzzles. Invite friends over or arrange a family game night.

You might realize you've been playing with the same toys and gadgets for a while. Are you ready for different ones? Toy and educational catalogs and websites are filled with all sorts of play materials you may not see in regular stores. Or look for toys, art supplies, or hobby materials at thrift shops and yard sales. Your dad or mom can ask friends and relatives to send along no-longer-used items that are still good. You never know what you might get: board games from the past, unique action figures or dolls, unused craft materials, and other cool stuff. Maybe you'll find something new to spark your interest and imagination.

If something you try isn't as fun as you expected, move on to the next play activity on your list. In a month or so, go back to the activity you didn't like. Give it a second chance—you might enjoy it this time.

Try Dramatic Play

One way to become more imaginative is to try dramatic play. Pretend to be a character or use an action figure or stuffed animal to act out a role. When you do this, you suddenly have to deal with *conflict*—like, the villain wants to take over the world and the hero must save the day. You have to react and be creative to keep the story alive. That's the power of play. It's practice for the real world, even if you never meet an evil villain or fly through the skies wearing a cape.

Do you spend time each day pretending or doing dramatic play? Sometimes, kids with ASD don't do enough of these activities. Maybe pretending doesn't come as naturally to you. Or perhaps you missed opportunities to be in childhood play groups where imaginary play was the main event. A need for play still lies within you. Let it out!

Max's Story

Max is 8 years old. His autism severely affects his ability to communicate and be social. One of the best ways Max's family helps him is through something they're all good at: play.

When Max was younger, his family used to set up play-dates with "typical" kids in the neighborhood. They'd play Grocery Store, using pretend food, a grocery list with PECS* pictures, and fake money. Max's job was to ask for each item on the list (to get him to talk more), pay for the food, and take it home. But for fun—and to help Max—his family would pretend that important ingredients were left off the list by mistake. Back to the grocery store Max went, over and over again, until all the ingredients were ready and it was time to "cook."

Soon Max's family decided to make the plot of the game more exciting. What might happen if a fire broke out in the store? (One of the kids became a "firefighter," with a red plastic hat, black boots, and an old kitchen-sink hose.) What if a robber held up the store? (A "police officer" with a cap and badge appeared to catch the bad guy.) What if the robber escaped from jail? (Max to the rescue!)

In a fun, creative way, Max was learning to adjust to the movement, noise, and changes that naturally happen as kids play. Best of all, he got to be part of a group of other kids his age, where he was the focus of attention. All the while, Max's family took photos of the play sessions. His mom collected them into social stories—homemade books that showed the order of what took place. Later, Max could look at the books to remember the fun he had.

Now that he's older, Max's family is working with his school to bring play and social time into his day. During one gym class per week, Max goes to a classroom with other kids who volunteer to play with him. Max's mom and the speech teacher help direct activities that teach Max social skills through play. This week the activity is about trains because Max loves trains.

Max loves the day at school. So do the other kids. They can't wait to find out what will happen next week when the social group gathers again.

*PECS stands for Picture Exchange Communication System—sets of pictures used for visual communication.

Ways to Be More Playful

- Play with a younger brother or sister, or a neighbor. Little kids love to pretend. They'll dress in costumes, make dolls "talk," build creative structures, or act out scenarios you come up with.

- Ask a parent or an older sibling to play with you for a specific length of time every day. Teens and adults may be a bit out of practice when it comes to pretend play. They still might surprise you by acting silly or telling you in an excited voice, "I remember when I had a robot like this!" Together, you can invent, make up stories, and discover your playful sides.

- Watch what other kids your age do for fun. Are there certain games your classmates do during recess? Do kids in the neighborhood gather at a local park or playground? Can an adult set up a play group or club for kids your age who have ASD or who share similar interests? (For more on this, see page 76.)

- Ask if you can get involved in community theater or a drama club at school. Being part of a theater group allows you to pretend in a way that's more scripted. (Having a script and a coach or director can help if you're not used to dramatic play or acting.) Along the way, you may learn about performing, building sets, putting together costumes, and even singing and dancing.

- Use play as a way to practice real-life scenarios. For example, how would your action hero handle someone who bullies? How would your stuffed animal throw a party? If you were a pretend teacher, how might you help your students learn about other places and cultures? When you play it, you live it. And that helps you make connections to the real world.

- Add imagination to everything you do. If you're sledding, pretend you're a penguin or that you're on a luge (that fast sled you see in the Winter Olympics). If you're in the pool, be a fish, a mermaid, or Aquaman. If you're giving friends piggy-back rides, make them pretend to buckle their seatbelts or give you a ticket first. Play together using funny voices. Crack jokes, put on weird costumes or outfits, sing, dance, and have a good time.

I build with Legos. I like to construct cities. I like to design buildings and worlds of my own. I also like to make movies of them.

—14-year-old boy

Great Ways to Spend Your Time

Abby loves making friendship bracelets. She learned how to weave colorful threads into bracelets one year at a summer camp for kids with ASD. Because Abby has a good memory, she could look at a pattern and then make a bracelet without reading all the instructions. Soon she started making bracelets all the time. She gave them to her friends and classmates. This almost led to some trouble at school when Abby was making bracelets instead of doing her work. But her teacher came up with an idea. She said that if Abby agreed to make bracelets only at home, she could bring them in to sell at the school store. Now kids at school can buy the bracelets to give to others. Abby feels great because she's not just a bracelet maker but also a "businesswoman."

Arno realized that team sports weren't his thing. He tried activities like tennis and gymnastics, but they took a lot of coordination. He wanted an activity that got him outdoors but didn't lead to frustration. Then he remembered something he loved: *fishing*. His grandfather started taking him fishing in his boat when he was a lot younger, and Arno was good at it. He decided that fishing could be his sport. Now Arno has a journal he takes with him every time he's on the boat. He records the date, his location on the lake, and how many fish he catches. Then he leans over the side of the boat and takes a photo of the water. When other people see his photos, they see only water. But for Arno, those pictures bring back every detail—the rod and reel, the bait, the sky, the smell of the air, and most of all, the fish!

Like Abby and Arno, you might have something in your life that brings you feelings of happiness and satisfaction. Maybe it's an activity, a hobby, a collection, or a game. Having intense interests is part of your ASD—but it's also a part of *who you are.* Find ways to pursue your interests, because they give you something to *do.* They help you think, dream, relax, and express yourself.

Think of ways to include others in your special interest. Then you'll have something in common with other people. Could you:

- Teach a classmate to play the game you love?
- Find other kids who collect the same things you do?
- Invite siblings or cousins to do your hobby with you?

What if you don't have a special interest yet? Or you want new ideas for fun ways to spend your time? Try these ideas:

Sign up for an activity. Does your school offer extracurricular activities you're interested in? There might be academic clubs, band, orchestra, choir, chess club, the yearbook or newspaper, or something else. Get involved! If there isn't a club that appeals to you, what about starting a small one with a couple of friends? Some kids start book clubs or clubs based on special interests, like games or cards for collecting.

Try athletics and sports. Check out what your school has to offer, or look for programs offered at the YMCA/YWCA or your local community center. Learn skating, karate, archery, swimming, or golf. At home, stay active by playing outdoors, jumping rope, dancing, stretching, running around, or walking the dog. You can read more about the importance of physical activity in Chapter 21.

Get creative at home. Instead of spending too much time in front of the TV or computer or playing video games, do something that takes more imagination. Sketch your self-portrait. Invent a comic strip. Make collages. Write stories and poems. Teach yourself the different forms of solitaire. Take photos of family and friends, or make home videos. Keeping your mind and hands busy is a great way to increase your creativity.

Join a scouting program. Scouting programs are set up to teach kids about fitness, responsibility, and good character. You'll learn to camp and hike, do fun activities with other kids, and take part in volunteering. You can learn more about scouting through your school or by going online with a parent.

Take a Look!

Are video and online games the thing you love to do more than anything else? Think of ways to expand this interest beyond the screen. Can you draw the game's characters? Go outside with a friend and pretend to be the characters? Build an outdoor obstacle course that resembles the game's different levels? Use your imagination!

Take lessons. Music, acting, singing, painting, photography, martial arts—whatever interests you, give it a try. Maybe a teacher can come to your home. Or maybe you can take lessons at a place that includes kids of different abilities. You might discover a special talent, and you'll see that building new skills can be challenging *and* fun.

Explore the arts. Attend your school's plays, and go to the plays and musicals that the local high school puts on. Show up for your school's concerts (choir, band, or orchestra). In your community, go to free concerts, shows, museums, and galleries. All of this helps create an interest in art, music, theater, and performance—works of the imagination!

Volunteer your time. Does your school have a service club? If it does, join up. School service clubs are a great way to be part of the community and help people in need. Another option is to participate in volunteer activities through a church, synagogue, mosque, or other place of worship. Does your dad or mom volunteer? Maybe you could go along to see what it's like and offer your help. When you give your time and assistance, you feel good about yourself. You see that other people have problems too. You start to see that, as human beings, we can boost each other up and make a difference.

Act out stories. Turn your closet or room into the setting from your favorite book or comic series and become characters from the stories. Or, you can write mysteries, set up pretend crime scenes, hide some clues, and watch your friends and family become detectives on the case. Another option is to reenact famous battle scenes from history books or to pretend you're people from another place and time.

Form a social group. You'll need some help from a parent or another trusted adult to make this happen. It's worth it! Call it whatever you like—a play group, social skills club, friends club, or something you make up. The goal of each gathering should be having fun. Perhaps the group will always meet at your home, or you'll take turns hosting. Plan for about two hours of fun. Make sure you have games, toys, activities, and things to do. Try to organize something that involves everyone, so it truly is social time.

Playing with other kids your age—especially in a group of three or more—helps you learn to get along with others. In group play, the rules and ideas may change quickly, and you'll learn to adjust to that. Plus, you'll keep fine-tuning social skills such as sharing and cooperation. A group like this can help you build friendships too.

Over time, members may come and go, and you might decide to include new kids in the group. Maybe you'll meet after school once a week. Maybe you'll gather two weekends each month. See what works for everyone involved.

Summers are an especially good time to start a social group or to increase the amount of time your current group spends together. Why? Because summer days are *unstructured*—they don't have a plan the way school days do. As a person with ASD, you probably need structure to stay organized and interested. Without school, many kids with autism spectrum disorder simply don't have enough to do—they get restless and bored. Having a planned social activity written on the calendar is important!

Chapter 10

Good Communication:
Body Language and Listening

One of the main symptoms of autism spectrum disorder is a difficulty with communication. You might have trouble understanding other people, reading or writing, and using language to express your feelings. This isn't because you aren't "smart"—it's a difference in how your brain is wired.

Your brain tends to see things in smaller parts, instead of being able to focus on the whole picture. Your brain may also have a slower processing speed. This means it takes you longer to gather information and put what you have learned into words. In spite of these challenges, you can learn and practice communication skills.

3 Tools for Learning Good Communication

For best results, you'll need three things: a crew (group) of communication helpers, a video camera, and time to practice every day.

Communication crew. Find an adult who can help you with the activities in this chapter: your mom or dad, a grandparent, or another caregiver. This person is like your "crew leader," who helps guide you through the activities and works with you to improve your skills.

It's also helpful to have peers you can practice with. How about brothers, sisters, cousins, neighbors, classmates, friends, or a social skills group? (Read more about social groups on pages 76–77.) Why is it important to practice with other kids? People your age have unique ways of communicating with each other. By watching other kids and doing what they do, you learn to communicate in these special ways. Plus, you get a chance to be social.

If you have a speech therapist, this person can be part of your crew too. Let your therapist know about what you're working on at home. Then, together, you can figure out ways to make your speech sessions even more effective.

Video camera. Does your family have a video camera or smartphone that can take videos? Or, could you borrow one from relatives? If so, you can record your practice sessions and family conversations and then watch them later. This is an excellent way to see where you need help.

Sometimes, when you start building a new skill, the other ones you've learned may fall by the wayside. For example, you might start with eye contact and make a lot of progress. But then when you move on to listening skills, you may be concentrating so hard on them that you forget to include eye contact as well. This is why it's helpful to have videos to watch. You can go back to one of your older videos and quickly see, "Oops, I forgot to *look* at the person I was listening to."

Keep the videos—don't delete them or record over them. Someday, years from now, you may want to look back to see just how far you've come.

Regular practice time. You can try working on communication skills for about a half hour each day. Or do more if you want to! The amount of time you spend is up to you and your family.

Just be sure to give yourself *plenty of time* to build each new skill. It may take weeks, months, or even years to really get the hang of using eye contact regularly or listening more closely, for example. Take the time you need—it's not a race. After all, you're working on skills to last a lifetime.

Body Language

Did you know that our bodies "talk" without saying a word? That's known as body language. Lots of things go into body language: posture, gestures, eye contact, facial expressions, and even the distance between people.

Posture and Gestures

Posture—the way we stand—"says" something. If we're standing straight and tall, this might show that we feel alert or proud. If we're slumped over, we might be bored or tired. We use our hands to make gestures: we point out sights we want others to see, or motion for someone to come closer.

We might tap our feet when we're impatient. Or shrug our shoulders when we don't know the answer to a question. Or give a huge yawn when we're sleepy. Closed fists can show anger. Folded arms can say we don't like what we're hearing. So can a stomping foot, a grunt, or a sigh of impatience.

Take a Look!
This chapter focuses on the *nonverbal* aspects of communication. (*Nonverbal* means *without words*.) You'll learn about body language, eye contact, and better listening. Then, in Chapter 11, you can read about another important aspect of communication: *verbal skills,* or using words.

High fives

Fist bumps and knuckle bumps

Pointing to something to make someone else look

Hand motions to say "Come here"

Waving hello and good-bye

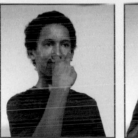

Pointing to the eyes, with two fingers, to say "I'm watching you"

Thumbs up to say "Good job" or "Well done"

All of these postures and gestures are forms of communication. Without saying a word, we've "told" people something about what we think or feel.

As a person with ASD, you might have trouble "reading" body-language and facial-expression clues like the ones just described. Perhaps you don't notice the clues. Or maybe you spot them, but don't know what they mean. Sometimes, you might not be able to see the whole picture—you see "parts" of the person's body or face but can't put them together quickly or at all.

Because of your ASD, you have two communication challenges:

- reading other people's body language
- using body language yourself

Remember, practice is the key. Start by noticing the different gestures the people around you use, especially kids your age.

Sometimes, kids who have ASD have trouble with gestures. Ask someone to show you how to do the motions correctly, and practice until they look (and feel) more natural.

Then use the gestures, when appropriate. Wave to people when you say hi or bye, for example. Practice pointing with your index finger (instead of using another finger to point). Give high fives when someone wins a game or makes a great play. All of this helps you connect each skill to your daily life, which is so important!

Eye Contact

Eyes can tell a lot about what a person is feeling or thinking. Someone's eyes might have a faraway look, or be brimming with tears, or nearly "sparkle" with excitement. These clues reveal emotions that may not always come across in the person's words.

Next time you talk to someone, pay special attention to where you focus your eyes. Do you look at the person—or do you look at an object in the room? If you look at the person, which part are you focused on: Eyes? Mouth? Head? Shoulders? Another body part? Maybe you tend to look at the person's mouth. Many people with ASD look at the mouth, instead of the eyes, when people are talking.

Making eye contact is an essential communication skill. That may not seem fair to you. Why should there be some rule about looking people in the eye when it makes people on the autism spectrum so uncomfortable? But if you *don't* look at people's eyes, you miss out on a lot of nonverbal communication. The eyes can tell you about a person's emotions. They can let you know if the person is paying attention to you. And what if someone's eyes are looking in another direction, or rolling whenever you say something? That's a big clue that you don't have the person's attention.

Here are a couple tricks to use if it's hard for you to look at people's eyes:

- Look at the forehead instead. Choose a point right at the top of the person's nose, low on the forehead. Then it won't seem as if you're studying the person's hair.

- Try a technique of "brief glances." As you talk or listen, glance into the person's eyes for a second, then look away. Continue to glance and look away again. By meeting the person's eyes, even for just a moment at a time, you connect. And that's what eye contact is about—*making a connection.* In our social world, these connections are crucial.

Just to be clear, eye contact doesn't mean staring. If you stare at someone closely, that will make the person feel uncomfortable. Sometimes, staring can even be taken as a threat. It's important to practice eye contact that makes others feel comfortable. Get out the video camera and have someone record you speaking with another person. Watch the video afterward to see where your eyes were looking. Did the eye contact seem natural? Did you look at the other person frequently, without staring too hard? Did you feel yourself making a connection?

Being able to make eye contact helps you make friends. Other kids will see your interest in them and they'll take more interest in you. Making eye contact with your teachers will help you seem like an eager learner, or at least someone who's trying hard. Later on in life, eye contact will even help you in job interviews. It's a skill worth working on, even if it's difficult. Be patient with yourself.

Facial Expressions

Facial expressions are another form of nonverbal communication. The human face can express so many feelings: anger, fear, embarrassment, sadness, worry, joy, excitement, curiosity, boredom, satisfaction. Sometimes, a person's face can flicker from one expression to another so quickly that it's hard to keep up.

| angry | scared | sad |
| excited | confused | bored |

To make matters more confusing, the expression on someone's face can hide the person's true feelings. For example, your mom might be sad one day, but if she doesn't want you to know that, she could force herself to smile and pretend everything's okay. Or, your brother could tease you by putting a frightened expression on his face, pointing to something behind you. You might turn quickly, thinking something really awful is creeping up on you, only to discover nothing is there. Your brother's expression fooled you!

Here's an example of "misreading" body language: Suppose you have something important to tell your dad, and you find him at the kitchen table paying bills. At first, you don't notice that he has a frustrated expression on his face. He's rubbing his head. He's looking down at his calculator. You might think this is a good time to talk because your dad is quiet. But the moment you speak, your dad says, "Can't you see I'm busy here?" Chances are, you missed some important clues about his mood:

- His face was saying "I'm frustrated."
- His hands were rubbing his head. Maybe that meant he had a headache or was thinking really hard.
- His eyes were looking down, probably because he was concentrating and didn't expect to be interrupted.

It's not your fault if you miss clues like these. That's part of having ASD. As you get older and keep working on communication skills, you'll read these clues more easily. You'll learn ways to watch for signals that tell you, *without words,* what another person might think or feel.

Your own facial expressions communicate to others too. It's been said that some people with ASD have a blank look. (This is another way of saying "not much facial expression.") Maybe this describes you. If so, then it's probably difficult for other kids to imagine what you might be thinking or feeling. They may even get the impression that you're not thinking about much at all. *You* know your mind is filled with interesting thoughts, dreams, and feelings—but other people may not.

Here's something you may not realize: Many "typical" kids spend a lot of time looking in mirrors to check themselves out, especially when they're preteens or teens. They stare at their reflection, making all sorts of expressions—mad, glad, sad. It's almost like they're posing for a camera. Many younger children do this too. They discover how they look as they make different faces or imitate other people. "Typical" kids of all ages also study photos of themselves, trying to figure out if they're attractive. Chances are, you haven't done a lot of this yourself. It's possible that faces simply don't hold as much interest for you.

As humans, we look at faces as we communicate. We do this to try to understand another person's thoughts and feelings. We listen to the person's words, but we also concentrate on the eyes and expressions to see if the person seems truthful or to make sure we really understand. This ability to read faces is like a built-in navigation system (like GPS) that "typical" people are born with. If you don't have the same system, you get lost more often when it comes to communication.

This means you need to create your own navigation system if you want to get

better at communication. Start by working with an adult to become more familiar with different facial expressions and the emotions they express:

- Look at faces in magazines and try to identify people's feelings.
- Together, take photos of family members making "emotion faces." Then label them with the matching feelings: shy, happy, anxious, furious, sneaky, giggly, mad. Place these photos in an album you can look at again and again.
- With a parent, go online to look for posters, books, apps, and other tools designed to help kids with ASD recognize facial expressions.

At home, practice making pleasant expressions you can use when you're speaking with people. Smile in different ways—with your teeth showing or your lips closed. Try to look relaxed and approachable, but not "blank." We're not suggesting that you go around with a fake smile! Just become more aware of your facial expressions and what they might say to people. This is where taking a video comes in handy. A parent can record what you look like when you're talking to friends and family. When it's your turn to listen, do you look interested? When it's your turn to talk, do you change your facial expressions to match what you're saying?

School is a good place to practice paying more attention to faces. There, you're surrounded by kids of all ages who look different and whose expressions are always changing throughout the day. Pretend you're a spy, gathering information about what people might be thinking or feeling. Notice when different classmates seem annoyed, pleased, or confused. At the lunch table, look around as you eat, watching how the other kids interact. Can you tell, just from facial expressions, who likes their lunch and who doesn't? Or who's having a good day and who's not? What more can you learn from what you see?

Let your friends help you get better at reading their thoughts. Every so often, you might say, "You look excited. Did something good happen?" Or "You seem sad. What's up?" If you notice an expression on your friend's face and wonder what it means, speak up. You could say, "What are you thinking right now?" This is a step toward *good communication*.

Plus, you get to learn from real-life situations, which is even better than practicing skills at home.

Personal Space

People like to have some personal space around them during conversations or when standing in line. There are rules, often unspoken, about what is considered a polite distance. Have you ever been in a situation where another kid at school says, "You're too close to me" or "Back up"? Maybe you didn't realize you had crossed a boundary—because it's an invisible boundary! You can't *see* it, so you have to *sense* it. But having ASD can make it difficult to sense those boundaries.

Imagine that each person is contained within a clear bubble. The unspoken rule is that other people shouldn't get inside that space—unless they're family or very close friends. If it's hard for you to picture an imaginary bubble, try this: Put your arm straight out in front of you. Where your fingertips are right at this moment is an *arm's length away*. That's a good distance to put between yourself and your classmates. Now you're setting personal boundaries that help you and the people you talk to feel more comfortable.

If you tend to get very close to people when you speak to them, they may back up. Watch for that clue (the backing away). It tells you you've accidentally gotten inside their "bubble." Other kids at school might be direct enough to say, "Can you move back?" But if they're not, it will help if your teacher knows you're working on personal-space issues. Ask your teacher to give you a secret signal that tells you

Take a Look!

Personal space can be a big issue when playing with other kids. Sometimes, play gets rough (like when you're racing, wrestling, or having pretend battles). During those times, the personal-space boundary doesn't seem to apply. But it actually does! There are **rules about not getting too rough.** There are also rules about **knowing when to stop.**

ASD can make the rules harder to understand. For example, you may tag or hit people too hard but not realize it. What feels like a light touch to you could feel like a smack to someone else. How confusing! Talking to an expert on sensory issues can help you better understand how this works.

Sometimes, during rough and active play, you might miss some of the signals your friends are sending. For instance, you and your buddies might shout so loudly during a wrestling match that you don't hear someone yell, "Stop! That hurts!" Or, you might tickle a friend to make him laugh and not realize that you're tickling too hard.

It's important to have fun—but also to know when the fun has stopped. A parent can help you become more aware of whether you're being too rough with friends and siblings. You could make up a signal for all of you to use, like forming your hands into the shape of a letter T to say "time out." Whenever someone uses that signal, it's a clue to stop, take a few deep breaths, and step back. Instead of physical play, move on to something quieter, such as art or a board game.

if you're overstepping a boundary. Your teacher could tap you on the shoulder and whisper a word like "bubble." Or your teacher could draw a circle shape in the air to let you know you need to back up.

With family members, standing or sitting close isn't usually as much of an issue. Unless, of course, it's an issue for *you.* Maybe you sometimes feel uncomfortable if your siblings or parents get too close to you. They may not even realize that you need a little distance at times. Let everyone at home know what you've learned about a need for more personal space. You can use hand signals at home too: You might draw a circle in the air or use a gesture your family makes up. You might also decide on a family phrase you all agree on, such as "Please give me some space."

With close friends—kids you frequently spend time with at your home or theirs—the personal-space issue gets a little trickier. Often, friends don't require as much distance during conversation or play. In fact, you might sit close to each other while you play games, do art, or talk. It all comes down to what you and your friends prefer.

If you need more personal space, you could say it in a friendly way: "I'm backing up a little because I need some space. No offense, okay?" Or, "I'm having one of those days where I need some personal space. Do you mind if I sit over here for a while?" (Then move to a chair or a different area of the floor.) If you tend to be the one who gets a little too close, let your friends know you're working on it. Show them the circle signal, which they can use to quietly say, "Back up a little, please."

Learning to Listen

Do people have trouble getting your attention? Do they usually call your name several times before you notice? Do they say stuff like "Pay attention, please!" or "Did you hear anything I just said?" Many people on the spectrum find it challenging to tune in and listen. Or, they may be listening quite well but aren't showing it in a way that other people understand.

Listening is an essential part of good communication. You have to listen carefully to:

- follow instructions
- learn what you're being taught in school
- do what your parents ask you to do
- get along with siblings at home
- make friends and have lasting relationships

Adults are often pretty good at being patient with someone who has ASD. For example, your mom or dad is probably used to calling your name a few times before you respond. Your teacher might know you have a condition that affects your ability to communicate, and so will make accommodations for you at school. The adults on your team (see Chapter 7) realize you need more time to listen to the directions you're given at appointments, so they'll take extra time to explain things carefully.

But guess what—*kids* often aren't as patient. If other kids get the feeling you aren't listening, they might simply walk away. If they don't know how to get your attention, they'll probably give up after one or two tries. Other kids may not realize you have ASD. If they don't understand you and your special needs, they might not make much of an effort—and they'll miss out on getting to know you. They shouldn't miss out on this chance, because you're worth getting to know!

You don't *have* to tell other kids, "I have some trouble with communication, so I hope you can be patient with me." But you *can* if you want to. Sometimes, giving other kids information about ASD can help.

You could say, "Sometimes I forget to look at people when they're talking" or "If it ever seems like I'm not listening, just tap me on the shoulder or say my name a little louder. That will get my attention." Then, instead of thinking you don't listen or you don't want to be friends, other kids might realize, "There's a difference here, and now I know what to do." That opens a door to friendship.

Eyes Listen Too

Listening with your eyes is often as important as listening with your ears. Focus your eyes on other people when they're speaking—even if eye contact is difficult for you.

How to Be an Active Listener

The rule is you should face the person you're listening to. Turn your body toward the speaker, focus your eyes on the person's face, and nod your head every so often. Nodding shows that you're taking in the information.

Remember all you read about eye contact and facial expressions? Now is the time to use what you've learned. When other people are talking, try to look as if you're actively listening:

- Keep your eyes focused on the person's eyes or forehead.

- Smile when appropriate, and try to look interested.

- Make sure not to interrupt.

- Nod your head (or say "Yeah" and "Uh-huh" a few times) to show you understand.

> I have to work hard to pay attention to what is happening, because I have an auditory [listening] problem. I don't always catch what people say, or I can't follow, or I'm thinking of something else.
>
> —14-year-old boy

Learning to listen is a skill that *all* kids have to learn, not just kids with ASD. So you're definitely not alone when it comes to needing practice in this area!

Your family can help you and your siblings learn better listening skills by using a timer and a prop. The prop can be a hat, a stick or wand, a ball, or another object that can be passed back and forth. Sit together in a room and take turns talking, so you can all practice listening. The person who's talking should wear the hat or hold the stick, wand, or ball. No one can interrupt while the speaker is talking. When the timer goes off, it's the next person's turn to talk—the visual prop is passed to that next speaker. The prop is the tool that reminds everyone to stay quiet and be good listeners.

Next, figure out how well people listened. Go around the room, taking turns saying something about what each person spoke of and what was said. (Keep passing the prop, if you'd like.) Here's where it gets interesting. What did you notice? Was everyone paying close attention? Were you all able to remember what people said—or did some of you get confused along the way?

This is helpful information to know. If you have trouble remembering things you hear, then you might need more visual aids at school so you have a better chance of success. Your speech therapist might be able to suggest certain activities and skill-builders to help you improve in this area too.

Putting the Skills Together

After you've focused on using body language and active listening, you can work on putting the skills together. Combining the skills takes practice. You may need prompts and reminders from an adult—that's okay. You'll feel more comfortable once you've had time to run through the skills over and over. The more you can use them in daily life, the better. Get out the video camera and spend time recording conversations that take place at home. (Ask permission from the people who are talking.)

First, pay attention to the speakers. If you're handy with the camera, you can focus on each speaker's face when the person talks. Then pan out again to get a view of all the speakers. What do their facial expressions tell you? Can you identify people's emotions by the expressions on their faces? While talking, where do the speakers' eyes look? What are their hands doing? What do the different gestures mean?

At times, focus on the listeners instead of the speakers. Later on, watch the video with your family. Conversations aren't always easy to follow in the moment. But when you have one recorded, you can push *pause* whenever you'd like. You can rewind to go back and listen more closely or to watch how someone's facial expression has changed.

You might see all sorts of interesting clues that tell you what people are feeling and thinking.

- Do their voices get louder or softer, depending on their emotions?
- Does the conversation speed up and slow down at certain points? Is there a sort of natural rhythm to the conversation?
- Do the speakers interrupt each other? If so, what happens?
- What do different people's hands, body postures, eyes, and facial expressions tell you?
- Do you see some active listening going on? Do the listeners focus, nod, and seem interested?
- What do you notice about eye contact?
- Do the speakers seem to be making a connection? Why or why not?

The suggestions in this section—like all the ones in this chapter—aren't meant to be used only once. Do them again and again. It's almost like being an athlete in training: You have to keep doing the exercises (in your case, *communication* exercises) to make progress.

Your family and helpers can add their own original spin to any of the activities:

- A homemade prop can make listening more fun. How about a funny crown you decorate together?
- Create your own phrases about personal space. Maybe if someone is standing too close, you'll say, "Don't be a space invader!"
- Invite relatives and close family friends over for gatherings where you record conversations to listen to later. You might be amazed at the stories that come out. Some of these recorded conversations might even become family treasures.

Chapter 11

Good Communication:
Making Conversation

Conversations are complex forms of communication, even if the talk sounds something like this:

Person 1: "Dude."

Person 2: *"Duuuude."*

Person 1: "Can you believe that happened?"

Person 2: "Totally."

Person 1: "I know. He's out of control."

Person 2: "You said it."

Person 1: "Catch you later."

Person 2: "Cool."

If you overheard that, you might think, "what in the world are they talking about?!?" Sometimes two people say only a few words but still have an intense conversation. And messages come through what isn't being said. All sorts of nonverbal (without words) communication occurs. So much is expressed through gestures, tone of voice, and facial expressions. You can read more about that in Chapter 10.

But the *words* matter too.

One of the hardest things for kids with ASD is making conversation. Even if you started talking early in life and have a large vocabulary, you may find conversation challenging. In conversations, people interrupt and talk over each other. They change the subject unexpectedly. They have "inside jokes" only they understand, and use all sorts of slang words and nicknames. That's a lot to follow.

This chapter offers tips to help you become a better conversationalist.

It's likely that you're already working with a speech therapist at school or a special center—and that's great. Speech therapists are trained to help people learn communication skills. But it's also important to work on your skills at home as often as you can. Why? Because conversations happen at home every day, and it's a convenient place to practice.

Conversation: It's Complicated

Conversations have a back-and-forth rhythm, almost like a ball being tossed from one person to another.

Person 1: "Hey, how's it going?"

Person 2: "Okay. That test was so hard!"

Person 1: "Yeah. What did you put for number three?"

Person 2: "I think it was 100. What did you put?"

Person 1: "I don't remember, but I think I got it wrong. What's for lunch today, anyway? I'm so hungry!"

Person 2: "Some slimy casserole. I brought cold lunch."

Person 1: "You were smart."

Person 2: "Not smart enough to ace the test!"

When two people talk, they go back and forth, taking turns making statements and asking questions. That back-and-forth isn't as easy for you because of your difficulties with communication. When you add more people into the conversation,

Take a Look!

This chapter focuses on the *verbal* aspects of communication—using words. You'll learn about starting a conversation, asking questions, giving responses, staying on topic, and understanding tone of voice. In Chapter 10, you can read about the *nonverbal* (without words) part of communication. The 3 Tools for Learning Good Communication in Chapter 10 (page 78) will help you work on all the conversation skills in Chapter 11.

it can seem as if words are flying back and forth so fast you can hardly keep track. It's a challenge to follow the words and to know who's saying what. Then there's the body language, the facial expressions, the eyes flitting back and forth . . . confusing!

Like many kids with ASD, you may feel more comfortable with *monologue,* which means only one person is speaking (you). Maybe you can talk at length about topics that really interest you. You might even be a budding performer who can recite passages from books or movies, or tell funny stories and jokes you've memorized. These are great skills that can help you in life. But the goal of this chapter is to help you with *dialogue,* where two speakers do the talking.

Developing that back-and-forth conversational rhythm between you and another person is really important. It's the basis for friendships, classroom participation, and (someday) a job. Conversation is a form of *connection.* You reach out to someone by asking a question. That person reaches back by giving you an answer, and then asking you a question too. Back and forth, and back and forth. With every question and answer, you learn more about the other person, and that person learns more about you.

Tips for Starting a Conversation

So, how do you *start* a conversation? Sometimes, it's hard to know what to say. Maybe you're a little shy, and you hang back and don't say much. Or maybe you walk up to people and blurt stuff out, instead of letting a conversation begin in a smoother, more natural way. There are some basic "rules" for starting a conversation in a way that makes other people feel comfortable. Learning these rules will help.

Say hello. Greeting people when you first see them is a nice way to show you care and to help them feel welcome. Remember to say hi to the kids you sit by on the bus, and greet your classmates when you first get to school. Say hi again when you sit at the lunch table. Greet your family members too. It makes them feel good when you notice them. Saying good-bye when someone leaves is polite and caring too.

Learn people's names. Sometimes, kids with ASD have trouble remembering other people's names. If this is the case for you, spend some time looking through old yearbooks or class photos so you can match names to faces. Another idea is to ask a parent to take pictures of the kids in your class. Your parent can collect the photos and names in a book you keep with you. If you have a smartphone or a tablet, the pictures and names can go there too.

Pay compliments. Compliments are positive comments you make to another person. For example, you might compliment people on their appearance or on how well they played a game. A compliment can be as simple as "Nice haircut" or "Great job!" If someone compliments *you,* you can smile and say "Thanks."

Find a way to connect. There are lots of ways to start a conversation with someone. You could begin with a greeting: "Hi," "What's up?" or "How's it going?" Then you could add a compliment like "Cool shoes." Here's a greeting and compliment:

"Hi, Maria. I saw your artwork hanging on the bulletin board. It was so good!"

Another option is to make a comment. A comment is a simple statement about something you notice or have on your mind. Try comments like "That looks like a fun game" or "It sure is raining hard out there." Just make sure the comment actually fits the situation! Here are a couple:

"Hi. I heard we're having outdoor gym today and we get to play softball."

Or:

"Hey, Ethan, I saw that movie you were talking about yesterday. It was really cool."

Be sure to listen to the person's response! And then say something more to keep the conversation going.

Make a list of topics. If you can memorize a list of topics that kids commonly talk about, you'll be able to start a conversation more easily. Most kids talk about:

- school
- sports
- movies, videos, or television shows
- popular music
- pets
- food
- vacations
- favorite things

At home, practice what you've learned so far. Start with greetings. Say hi to family members when they come home and when they enter the room you're in. Next, work on compliments. Tell your dad what you liked about the meal he cooked, for example. Or let your sister know you like her new jeans. Your family will probably love hearing such nice things from you.

Try making more comments at home too: "Mom, I had a great day at school." Or "The weather looks pretty bad out there. I'd better bring a jacket." Maybe you don't usually say things like this because you believe that other people already know. But they don't necessarily know! Remember, just because you are thinking it doesn't mean other people are thinking it too. Your thoughts are separate from everyone else's.

By the way, try to keep your comments positive. Say something nice whenever you can, because people will respond in a friendlier way. Avoid saying things like "You have bad breath" or "You did terrible on that test." These comments may be true, but they could hurt someone's feelings.

The Next Level: Questions

Many kids with ASD have trouble with questions. Do you forget to ask people questions? Maybe it doesn't even occur to you to ask them. You might be used to finding answers in books or doing research online or on the computer. You probably love finding out facts or learning trivia! And you probably *don't* love learning about other people's opinions or emotions.

But questions connect you to other people in a powerful way. Most people like being asked questions about themselves. It makes them feel noticed and appreciated. This is a *great* skill to learn (in fact, it's an essential one). Asking questions of people you meet, and people you already know, is a way to reach out. You'll seem friendly, curious, and interested. And you'll be opening a door so that other people will ask *you* something too. That's how the back-and-forth begins.

Asking someone a question is one of the best ways to start a conversation. Here's an easy question: "How are you?" The person will probably answer "Fine. How are you?" If you're not used to asking this question when you see people for the first time each day, now is the time to practice. Start within your own family. When you wake up in the morning, try:

"Hi, how's it going, Mom?"

or

"Good morning, how'd you sleep last night, Grandpa?"

When you come home from school, ask:

"Hi, how was your day?"

Whenever someone else comes home, try a version of the same question:

"Hello! How's it going? What's new?"

Once these questions become a habit, you can practice other conversation starters:

"What are you thinking about?"

"Is that a good book?"

"What do you like about that game?"

"What did you do last night?"

"Are you going anywhere special today?"

Questions, questions, questions . . . keep asking them!

 I have trouble communicating, especially around a lot of people. Like, it's hard for me to say, 'What's up?'
—14-year-old boy

Responses

Once you're better at asking questions, you can focus on how you respond to questions others ask of you. Some kids who have ASD tend to keep their responses pretty short:

Parent: "Did you have a good day at school?"

You: "Yeah."

That conversation was stopped right in its tracks! Here's how to get a dialogue going:

Parent: "Did you have a good day at school?"

You: "Yeah. We learned about volcanoes. It was pretty cool. I want to learn more about them. How was your day?"

Parent: "My day was great—thanks for asking! Maybe you and I can look up some stuff on Pompeii later. Did you learn about Pompeii?"

See the difference? When you respond with more than a simple yes or no, a conversation can happen.

At home, practice adding a comment each time you answer with a yes or no:

"No, thanks, I don't want seconds—I'm full. Was that a new spaghetti recipe?"

Or:

"Yeah, I had art today and we did self-portraits. Did you do anything fun today?"

To get better at asking questions, listening to what the other person says, and giving responses, try this:

Practice talking on the phone. (You might be groaning right now. Lots of kids with ASD don't like talking on the phone!)

Talking on the phone (with no video) will give you a chance to concentrate on the conversation. You can close your eyes to block out distractions, and the other person doesn't have to know. (*Bonus:* You don't have to remember eye contact when you're on the phone.) If your phone has a volume control, you can turn it up to make sure you hear everything that's said.

For this exercise, practice with a family member. Talk together for a certain amount of time—maybe five minutes. Focus on asking some questions and answering the ones the other person asks you. Try to keep the conversation going so it doesn't "die" too fast. When the timer goes off, you might be ready to end the conversation—or let it continue if you're enjoying it. When you're ready to say good-bye, you can end with one of these statements:

"Well, it's been great talking to you!"

"I have to go now, but let's talk again soon."

"I'll talk to you later, okay?"

"Call me again sometime. Bye!"

Talking on the phone is a skill everybody needs to learn. Once you have the basics down, it gets easier—and so does conversation in general. You just might discover that asking questions isn't as hard as you thought. And your curiosity about other people will grow.

Talking on Topic

There's probably a subject or topic you love *so* much that you want to talk about it almost all the time: animals, football, stickers, video games, your collection, or whatever it may be. Sometimes, you might even interrupt conversations so you can talk about your favorite topic. Other times, you might forget to listen to people's questions or ideas because you're thinking of a way to bring up your best subject. This is known as talking off topic.

Notice how the conversation went from soccer to Pluto? In fact, this isn't actually a *conversation* in the true sense, because the people involved were talking about separate things. No real connection was made.

Your goal is to talk ON TOPIC. Why do you have to talk about other stuff if it really doesn't interest you? Because it's part of good communication. Think of communication as a two-way street: The traffic goes in two directions, not one. You need to pay attention to the other "drivers," because you share the "road" with them. They listen to you—and *you* listen to *them.*

At home, your family can give you little reminders, like "Talk on topic, please." That's your signal to pay closer attention to the conversation and participate in it—without going back to your familiar subject.

Another idea is to keep a timer in a handy spot at home. Then you can talk about your favorite thing for a limited time. A parent could say, "I know you want to talk about *Star Wars,* so let's set the timer for five minutes and I'll listen. But after that, you need to agree to change topics." After you've had a chance to talk about what interests you, you have to give the other person an opportunity to do the same. It's a good way to practice the back-and-forth aspect of conversation.

Remember that list of common kid topics on page 98? You might want to write down some questions to ask other kids to get a conversation started or to keep it going. If you have a list in your mind, you'll be ready to talk about things other than your favorite topic. Examples:

"Do you play a sport?"

"Seen any good movies lately?"

"Are you going on a vacation this summer?"

"What's your favorite activity?"

"Who's your favorite teacher?"

"What kind of music do you like?"

Listen to the person's response. Then say something ON TOPIC to keep the conversation going.

Does talking on topic mean you shouldn't *ever* talk about your favorite subject? Definitely not. You probably have lots of knowledge about whatever it is you love. You can share what you've learned with others. Just be sure that the people you're speaking with seem interested.

How will you know? They'll probably show the signs of active listening: They'll look at you, nod their head, and ask appropriate questions.

If someone is trying to get you to stop talking about a topic, the person might say one of these things:

"Cool. Can we change the subject?"

Or:

"Yeah. Want to go play a game or something?"

Or:

"Let's talk about something else."

Those are clues for you. You can then tell the person something like this:

"Sorry, I just realized I'm doing all the talking. What do you want to talk about?"

Or:

"Oops, I may be boring you. Want to talk about something else?"

Or:

"There I go again! I can get carried away when I talk about this topic. Let's change the subject."

Tone of Voice

In conversation, it's not only *what* you say that matters but also *how you say it*. People listen for clues that come through your tone of voice:

- Do you speak louder when you're excited? Do you talk softly if you don't want others to overhear?
- Do your words speed up when you get to the "good part" of the story?
- Do you pause when you want to make a point?
- Do you slow down your speech to emphasize certain words?

- Do you sometimes change your voice to imitate someone else's speech?
- Do you phrase questions as *questions* by raising the pitch of your voice at the end of the sentence?

All of these clues are considered standard speech patterns. No matter what language is spoken, many of these patterns serve as hints about the *meaning* behind the words.

When you have ASD, your speech might not fit the usual patterns. You may speak in a monotone, meaning your tone of voice stays at the same level, almost as if you're giving a lecture. At times, you may speak too loudly or softly.

You can't help it if your way of speaking differs from many people's. But if you're interested in making some changes in how you communicate, it *is* possible to do.

It's best if you work with a speech therapist who's trained to help kids with a variety of communication issues. A therapist can work with you on the pace and rate of your speech, pronunciation, tone of voice, or problems with the constant repeating of words or phrases. Challenges like these require the help of a specialist who can work up a plan for you and give your parents ideas on how to help you at home.

Still, there's a lot you can do on your own to practice communication skills. Following are ideas you can use at home and at school.

Putting the Skills Together

Record yourself. There's a reason you keep seeing this suggestion. Recording is a really helpful tool in learning new communication skills. Have your dad, your mom, or another family member record you talking to someone. Use a video camera or smartphone. Later on, you can watch or listen to the recording together to find out what your conversation strengths and weaknesses may be. For example, are you good at sharing your knowledge about certain topics or listening to other people share theirs? Awesome, keep it up! But do you need help remembering the back-and-forth aspect of conversation? Maybe you interrupt or forget to ask questions. Well, now you have something to work on . . . so get started! Bring the recorded conversations to your speech therapist or counselor so they can help you practice too.

Talk during meals. The dinner table is a great place to practice conversation, because the whole family is gathered. Use this time to improve your conversation skills, your listening, and your ability to ask questions.

Here's an activity to try: Let each person talk for two minutes, using a timer if you'd like. After each person has spoken, the other people at the table get to ask questions about what was said. (You can pass around a prop if you have one. See page 92 for prop ideas.) Many families use mealtime to talk about their day. They discuss what happened at school or work, what they had fun doing, whether the day was "good" or "bad." Other families use conversation-starter cards, which offer prompts for interesting things to discuss. You can find cards like these at gift stores—or your family can create homemade ones. That way, the conversation goes beyond "How was your day?" into brand-new territory.

Practice talking during activities. This is more challenging than you might think. Your brain likes to focus on one thing at a time, or to concentrate deeply on something that interests you, like a game or puzzle. When you're playing, you probably don't like to stop and talk—and if you *do* talk, it's only about the game. What if, in the middle of the game, your friend asks you a question about school, or your sister starts cracking jokes? You probably find that pretty annoying! It's like you suddenly have to "switch gears," and that isn't easy for you.

Switching gears and doing more than one thing at a time are skills. You can build these skills through practice. One way to practice is to throw a ball back and forth to a family member while you talk about your favorite topic. Your brain and body suddenly have to do two different things at the same time. An activity like this helps you improve your coordination and rhythm. (Remember, conversations have rhythm!) Another way to practice is to work on talking during games—but *not about the game.* As you play, tell the other players about a test you took, a funny video you saw, or what you want to eat for lunch. This helps your brain focus on two different things at once, which is a great skill-builder.

The Last Word . . .

People in your life and on your team of helpers will keep pushing you to talk—even if it's really hard for you. They'll prompt you to say hello and good-bye. They'll ask you questions and expect answers. They'll tell you to speak more quietly or in less of a monotone. They'll even try to get you to talk about your feelings, or to stop talking about the same things over and over. At times, you might feel frustrated with all these demands.

Because these people care about you and your future, they're asking you to go beyond what's comfortable or easy. They know that *communication* is the key to so many things: Making friends. Having strong relationships with family. Succeeding in school. Pursuing what interests you. Feeling comfortable in the wider world. If you work hard to improve your communication skills, they'll get stronger and you'll grow more confident. Keep trying!

> ASD can be very challenging at times, but it also can make you see things in a new way. Take life one step at a time, and no matter how bad things get, never give up.
>
> —17-year-old girl

Chapter 12

Your Social Skills Survival Kit

On TV, there are reality shows where people are put into highly unusual situations to test their Survival Skills. For example, they'll be dropped into the wilderness with very few supplies. There, they must pass every test of their courage and skill until they're the last "survivor." (No one actually dies, though.)

In another show, contestants pair up in a race to an unknown finish line. The racers are placed in foreign countries and cultures. They may not know the language and still must find their way. Mysterious clues direct each step in the confusing journey. Teamwork helps—but it would all be so much easier with a map and compass or GPS.

Do you ever feel like one of these reality-show contestants, dropped into the middle of a puzzling environment where you're not sure what to do, what to say, or how to get along? So many new skills to learn. So many hard-to-follow clues. So much language to figure out. You know what would be useful? A special Social Skills Survival Kit to help you through this often-confusing, fast-paced world.

It's not an actual kit you can hold in your hands—more like one you imagine in your *mind.* It includes four important tools that give you information, skills, and support for surviving social situations and feeling confident. These are the tools that will help you find your way through the social world and survive tough situations. Use your imagination to picture your kit and each tool in it. Ask a parent or another trusted adult to be your partner—someone who can give advice, offer solutions, and stand by you when you're feeling lost.

Survival Tool #1:
Imaginary GPS Device

One of the challenges of ASD is how it affects your level of awareness. What does *that* mean? It means you don't have a built-in ability to know where you're going, how to get there, and what you might face along the way.

For example, you might need help remembering what day or time it is, what's on your daily schedule, and what tasks you're expected to complete. The adults in your life probably keep you focused. They might provide a visual schedule or prompt you about what comes next. Many kids with ASD rely on routines to help them feel prepared and safe. Sometimes, any kind of change in the routine is upsetting and confusing.

Often, life isn't as predictable as we'd like it to be. Schedules change. New people arrive on the scene. Rules we've come to count on don't always apply to every situation. That's when we end up feeling lost and worried. Maybe you feel this way a lot of the time.

One thing that helps is developing a greater sense of awareness about what's happening around you. Not what you *expect* to happen or what you *want* to happen—but what's *actually going on.* This means opening your eyes and your mind a little wider than usual.

Think of it as turning on your GPS, or Global Positioning System. Beep! Locating . . .

Look where you are at various times of the day, and then think about what the situation requires. Different settings mean different types of behavior. Your awareness tells you what you might need to do. Here are some examples:

Nick is getting in trouble at school for things he didn't realize were a problem. During class, his teacher often says, "Nick, this isn't the time for jokes." But the kids are laughing! Nick likes the attention, and he feels like he's making friends. Isn't this what his parents and therapists want—for him to make friends and have more fun?

Jessie likes having her buddy Ben over on the weekends. They're neighbors, and they have a lot in common. They like to build with Legos, collect rocks, and make elaborate sand castles in the sandbox. Sometimes, Jessie gets so involved in building her structures that she forgets to talk to Ben. Other times, she gets bored playing the same old things. Then she wanders away, looking for a new activity. Ben is left all alone. Soon Jessie's mom yells, "Jessie! Aren't you forgetting something important? You have a guest."

Hakim has occupational therapy on Thursdays at 6 PM. His therapist is Karen. Karen follows a certain routine: First she does therapeutic brushing on Hakim. Next come several skill-building activities. After that Hakim gets time on the swings. This is what Hakim is used to and what he expects. But when Hakim and his mom arrive one Thursday, they learn that Karen hurt her ankle and can't do the session. Another occupational therapist smiles at Hakim and says, "I'll be your 'Karen' today." Hakim hates this. Another lady can't be Karen! Standing in the waiting room, Hakim starts to cry hard. "No!" he says. "This isn't how it works." He runs out the door and makes it as far as the parking lot. There are lots of parked cars and moving cars, but Hakim doesn't care. All he wants to do is get away.

In these examples, Nick, Jessie, and Hakim weren't thinking about the setting—about where they are, why they are there, and who else is there. They could have been more *aware* of what's really going on. Can you think of some ways these kids could use their (imaginary) GPS to handle these situations more successfully?

For **Nick,** the setting is his classroom. That's a place where he could show better "student behavior." Instead of making jokes, he could pay attention to the teacher and listen harder. Because he likes to joke, and he seems to get a good response from other kids, he can save his humor for lunchtime. That's a better place for his comedy show!

Ben is **Jessie's** guest. When she has Ben over, she needs to remember to treat him like one. During playdates, she'll have to talk with Ben to make him feel welcome. If Jessie gets tired of an activity, she might say, "Hey, Ben, want to do something else instead? How about a board game?" Then she can listen to what Ben wants to do. Together, they can decide on an activity they both like.

Running out of the waiting room was dangerous for **Hakim.** He could have gotten hurt in the parking lot. It's understandable that Hakim was upset by the change of plans. Taking deep breaths might have helped. While Hakim was calming down, the other therapist might have been able to explain that she knew Karen's routine and could follow it. Hakim could have asked questions about what might happen. He might have said, "I'm nervous. What can I do to feel better?"

The imaginary GPS could help each of these kids be aware of what other people around them expect. That's an important social skill! With help from an adult, practice using your personal GPS. It's a helpful tool to fine-tune your awareness. Keep paying attention to where you are and who you're with at different times each day. This is what tells you how to act and react appropriately.

Survival Tool #2:
Handbook of Customs

Did you know that before a trip to a foreign country, many travelers look at a handbook to get helpful information about the people and places they'll see? Travelers need to know about all sorts of stuff:

- traditions, customs, and manners of people in the area
- the local rules and laws
- handy phrases from the language

You may not be a traveler. But sometimes you might feel like you're in a foreign country—where people speak quickly and behave in ways you're still trying to figure out.

It feels like kids are either mean to me
or they treat me like I'm invisible.

—11-year-old boy

Another way some people with ASD describe their experience of the world is "being from another planet." Perhaps you feel like an outsider in a world of insiders, at least some of the time. If so, you need a handy reference guide, one that can serve as a little handbook of social customs. Well, now you have one, right here, as part of your Social Skills Survival Kit. If you can memorize these customs and guidelines, you'll have an easier time in the social world.

Basic greetings. When you enter a room, or when someone else enters, say "Hello" or "Hi," or give a little wave. Do this at home, at school, and in places where you see people you know. Be sure to say good-bye when you or someone else is leaving too. You don't have to greet anyone when you're going into a store or walking around in your neighborhood, unless you see someone you recognize.

> If you like, write some of the ideas from this section in a small notebook. Then you can check your own personal handbook of customs when you need a reminder.

Formal greetings. When you're meeting someone for the first time, there are a few rules to follow. Stand up if you're sitting down. Smile politely. Look the person in the eye, at least for a moment. If eye contact is hard for you, here's a trick to help you remember. Think to yourself, "I wonder what color eyes the person has." Take a quick look and find out. (For more on eye contact, see page 82.) Then say, "Hi. My name is _____(your name). Nice to meet you."

Introductions. Sometimes you'll be in a situation where you have to introduce someone. For example, maybe you have a friend over, and then another friend comes over. If the two friends don't know each other, you can introduce them like this:

"Jaden, I'd like to introduce you to my friend, Lee. Lee, meet Jaden."

Or:

"Jaden, this is Lee. Lee, this is Jaden."

Awareness of your "audience." You don't have to be onstage to have an audience. The people around you at home, at school, and in your community are like an audience. They listen to your words and watch your actions. Because of your ASD, you may not always be aware that you're surrounded by others—people who think their own thoughts and feel their own feelings. You may often believe that your thoughts match everyone else's, but they *don't.* Each person has unique thoughts.

"Typical" kids have a built-in awareness of this. Even at a very young age, they figure out that they need to change their words and behavior to suit their audience. For example, one moment a young child might be acting silly with friends. But what happens as soon as a parent or teacher enters the room? The child will probably notice and stop the silliness. The moment the adult leaves, the child might go right back to being silly again.

Here's another example: A group of boys might be standing around talking about how girls "are girly" and "like stuff that's pink and sparkly." Even if some of the boys don't agree, they might nod their heads and go along with the talk, just to feel like they're part of the group. Then, the moment a girl comes by, all the boys might suddenly go quiet or change the subject so she doesn't hear what's being said. They realize the girl could be hurt or annoyed by their comments, so they quiet down. That's an awareness of their audience—even if it's a girl just walking by, who isn't part of the conversation at all.

People with ASD often need to work harder to gain the same level of awareness that many people already have. It takes practice to develop the skill. But you can do it! With an adult's help, you can work on adjusting how you talk depending on who you're talking to and where the conversation takes place. For instance:

If you spend time with young children . . .
you'll learn patience and how to speak more slowly and clearly.

When you're with people your own age . . .
it's appropriate to use more slang or to talk openly about your likes and dislikes.

If you're with a teacher . . .
you'll need to speak more politely, as a sign of respect.

How you talk in a library (in a whisper) . . .
is different from
how you might speak at a noisy sporting event (shouting to be heard).

So much depends on the listener or listeners around you. You'll need to learn ways to adjust your words and volume. You'll be developing "audience awareness," a skill you can use all your life.

Polite remarks. As a person with ASD, you're probably very honest. That's a great quality to have. Telling the truth is important, and so is saying what you think. If you're doing these things already, way to go! But in some cases, people with ASD are a bit too blunt. (*Blunt* means you say something abruptly, without thinking to tone down your words.) Here's an example of being blunt: "Your hair looks awful. Why did you get it cut that way?" You might be telling the truth, but your words could hurt someone's feelings. It's better to make *polite* remarks. For example, you could instead say, in a friendly way, "I see you cut your hair. Do you like it the new way?" Or you could skip mentioning the hair at all, and just say something else: "I like your green jacket" or "Did you think the homework was hard?"

You won't always know when you're being too blunt. This is why it's helpful to ask an adult to help you work on this issue. (Find a parent or ask someone on your team of helpers. You can read more about this team in Chapter 7.) Your helper can point out times when you're a little too blunt. This grown-up can then help you rephrase the words in a more polite way.

As time goes on, you'll probably start noticing other people's reactions to your words. You'll be able to better read their body language and facial expressions (see pages 80–89). These things can tell you a lot about the effect your words have.

Private thoughts. This relates to the idea of being too blunt (see previous page). Because of your ASD, you might speak your thoughts aloud at times when it would be better to keep them to yourself. *Lots* of kids have this problem, even if they don't have ASD. The words just come out, before they can be stopped. Then—*oops!*—there's trouble. Feelings get hurt, or someone ends up angry.

Keeping your thoughts to yourself is a skill that speech therapists and autism experts can help you with. Your dad or mom can help too. It takes practice. You'll need to work on knowing whether what you want to say is appropriate. Plus, you'll need help noticing if what you've said has caused hurt or angry feelings. All this takes time. As you grow older, you'll gain a better sense of what's appropriate and what isn't. Keep asking for help.

Saying you're sorry. Sometimes, you'll make a mistake or hurt someone's feelings. What can you do? Apologize! Two small words—"I'm sorry"—can make a big difference.

It takes courage to admit when you're wrong, especially after an argument. You may still be angry and upset, and those strong emotions may get in the way of saying you're sorry. Practice can help. With a parent or another adult, you can role-play different ways to apologize. Like this: "It's my fault, and I'm sorry." Or: "I'd like to apologize for what I did. Can you forgive me?"

Asking for help. What do you usually do when you're feeling lost and confused? Do you speak up? For example, if you're in math class and you're having trouble understanding something, do you raise your hand and let the teacher know? It's important to do that! In fact, it's a *skill.*

Admitting you need help isn't a sign of weakness. It doesn't mean you're not smart. Anyone can get lost or have difficulty understanding. But no one will know it's happening to *you* unless you say something. Raise your hand and say, "I'm confused about what you just said. Can you repeat it more slowly, please? Thanks."

You can use this skill in all sorts of situations, even conversations. In Chapter 11, you'll find many tips on communication skills. Even if you follow them all and practice often, there will still be times when you don't understand what someone's saying. When that happens, you can say, "Sorry to interrupt, but I'm having trouble understanding you. Can you please slow down or say it again?" You might feel a little awkward, but it's worth being honest about your confusion. Otherwise, you'll probably misunderstand the person, and that can lead to frustration.

Survival Tool #3:
Skills for Being Assertive

Even if you're by nature a peaceful person, and you don't like fights and arguments, they happen. Conflicts occur when people don't treat each other fairly. In conflict situations like these, an important conflict-solving skill is Speaking up. When you speak up for yourself in a strong but polite way, you are being assertive.

Sometimes a conflict can take you by surprise. For example, you could be playing a video game, and then one of your siblings marches into the room and says, "*My* turn to use the TV!" You didn't start the disagreement, but suddenly you're right in the middle of it. Other times, conflicts keep happening. Maybe your friend always wants to choose the game the two of you will play. Maybe your sister thinks she should always get to use the computer first because she's older. Or, perhaps one of your classmates looks at your schoolwork and copies it.

In each of these situations, you're not doing anything wrong, but you probably feel annoyed, frustrated, and cheated. Feelings like that are challenging. They make your day harder and can add to your level of stress. What should you do? You may be able to help yourself if you use assertiveness skills and speak up for yourself.

Chapter 8 (pages 63–65) talks about handling conflicts that come up at home using STOP THINK GO. You can also use that skill when you have conflicts with classmates or friends.

Here are some examples of speaking up assertively:

"Let's take turns choosing. That's more fair."

Or:

"I need to use the computer from 4:00 till 5:00 today to work on my project."

Or:

"Please don't copy my work. It's against the rules."

Sometimes, it's hard to speak your mind like this—but you can do it! Use a kind but firm tone. Practice at home with a parent. See if you can make your voice sound confident but not harsh. Usually, speaking your mind is more effective if you can make eye contact with the person too. (Read more about eye contact on pages 82–83.) If eye contact is hard for you, then work on using your voice until you're more confident about assertiveness skills. Later on, practice looking the person in the eye when you speak your mind.

Speaking up usually works, but not always. What happens if you say what you want, and the other person doesn't agree? In this case, you might have to stick up for yourself even more. Here's an example of how to do it:

You: "Please don't copy my work. It's against the rules."

Other person: "I wasn't!"

You: "I saw you look at my paper. I've seen you do this before. I won't let you keep copying me."
(Notice the word "I" here. When you use "I," your words sound calm and straightforward. If you say something like "*You* looked at my paper" or "*You* are a big cheater," the other person is likely to feel accused and get angry.)

Other person: "Oh, yeah? What are you going to do to stop me?"

You: "If I see you copying me again, I'll report you to the teacher."
(Stay calm. Let the other person know you'll get adult help, if needed.)

Other person: "You're a jerk."

You: "Please leave me alone."

(If someone calls you a mean name, this doesn't mean it's true! Don't let yourself get caught in a name-calling contest. Instead of calling the person a name back, say that you want to be left alone.)

Other person: "Whatever!"

Even if the person stops doing what angered you in the first place, you'll probably feel upset after a disagreement. Take some deep breaths. If you're at school, you might need to take a break somewhere safe, like the resource room, media center, or front office. Talk to your teacher about what you might do to calm down and feel better. You can also look at Chapter 19 for other ideas to help you calm yourself.

Sometimes, people start shouting if they disagree. When this happens, the conflict gets worse instead of better. It's important to always try to speak up for yourself in a strong but *polite* way. This is a verbal skill all kids need to learn, not just those with ASD. Practice using a firm, strong voice, but don't yell.

Other times, people who are in arguments use their hands instead of their words. That's when the hitting, pushing, and punching start. Physical violence is never a good solution. If a disagreement with someone starts to get out of control, use your *feet* and walk away. Get help from an adult you trust.

Survival Tool #4:
Bullying Radar

Sheila dreaded going to school each day. Another girl was making Sheila a target. The girl would whisper mean words like, "You smell," "Here comes Sheila the Stupid," and "Why don't you just go home so no one has to look at you?" Sheila was surprised at how those quiet words rang loud in her mind, over and over, long after they'd been spoken.

Andre had a similar problem. A boy named Tate just wouldn't leave him alone. Tate and his friends would come up to Andre when no teachers were around, and they'd call him "Psycho" and "Andre the Giant." Even though Andre was tall for his age, the other kids weren't scared of him. They knew it didn't take much to make him cry. Sometimes, they flicked his cheek with their fingers or tried to trip him in the hall.

Theo, a fifth grader, wanted to be liked and admired. After joining the soccer team, he thought he had a group of instant friends. Some of the other guys on the team liked to make jokes and pull pranks. The guys were funny and they made Theo laugh. But sometimes, things went too far. They'd snap the waistband of his shorts and bounce the soccer ball off his forehead. Sometimes, Theo's teammates would tell him to go sniff a girl's hair or stand up in the lunchroom and do a huge burp. When he did these things, other kids laughed. For a while, Theo thought all of this was part of friendship and fitting in. But one day, his coach took him aside and asked Theo if he knew the difference between kids' laughing *with* him and laughing *at* him. Theo thought about the coach's words all day and realized he didn't like being the victim of jokes and pranks. He decided that he'd be more careful about letting his teammates take advantage of him.

In each of these situations, someone is being bullied. Bullying is when a person or group of people hurt, scare, or embarrass another person on purpose over and over again. The person being bullied has trouble defending themselves. You probably already know that bullies tend to push, shove, hit, punch, and insult others. But not all bullying is easy to identify. This is why you need bullying radar. It helps you tune in to a kind of bullying that's a bit harder to understand.

Diego's Story

New schools are hard—so many unfamiliar faces, classes, and teachers. Twelve-year-old Diego knows all about having to start over in a new place. Right now, he's in a small private middle school. He had started sixth grade at the public middle school, like all his friends and classmates from fifth grade. But that school was so big! Diego was overwhelmed by its size and by having to change classrooms for each subject. Partway through the year, his parents helped him switch schools. They found a place that was smaller, quieter, and easier to get around in.

But now that he's here, Diego is having a hard time. At his other school, the kids knew about his autism. Not everyone was nice to him, but he had friends. Now those friends seem so far away. Diego wanders the hallways of his new school, watching other kids talking and laughing. He feels lonely.

The kids at Diego's new school aren't used to having a student with autism in their classes. They don't seem to understand that when Diego gets upset he may talk too loud or flap his hands. The kids give him strange looks.

Diego realizes there are many good things about the new school. It's quieter and he knows what to expect. The classes are small, and the teachers treat Diego well. But, even so, Diego's organizational skills seem to be getting worse. Just yesterday afternoon, his favorite pen went missing. This morning, his science folder wasn't in his locker where he'd left it. And now his lunch is gone! All the kids are on their way to the cafeteria, but Diego is at his locker feeling confused.

He decides to go to the front office to call his mom. He tells her he forgot his lunch at home. "No, you didn't, Diego," says his mom. "I saw you walk out the door with it. Did you leave your lunch on the bus?"

"Maybe," Diego answers. "But I'm pretty sure I put it in my locker. The locker doesn't have a lock, Mom."

Someone must have taken Diego's lunch. He doesn't want to believe that. But what about the other items that seem to have disappeared?

The trouble doesn't stop there. Friday at the end of the school day, Diego goes to his locker to get all his stuff. To his surprise, the locker is empty. There's nothing there but some dust. Where are his books? His supplies? His gym shoes? Diego can't help it—he starts to cry.

The other students hurry to their buses, and Diego is left behind. He returns to his classroom and tries to find his missing stuff. No luck. He goes through the hallways, still looking. His belongings are nowhere to be found. What should he do? Call his mom? Then he realizes he's missed the bus! The halls are empty. Diego sits down in front of his locker and puts his head on his knees.

That's where his mom and the principal find him later. Diego's mom hugs him. "I was so worried when you didn't get off the bus with the other kids! What happened?"

Diego tells her about the mystery of the disappearing stuff. "It's not my fault, Mom. I didn't lose my stuff. Someone took it."

"Of course it's not your fault, Diego," his mom replies.

Diego's mom and the principal find a custodian who can help Diego search for his belongings. "While you're doing that," says the principal, "your mom and I can go have a talk in my office. We're going to solve this bullying problem. You need to feel safe at school, Diego."

Diego is relieved. He's even more relieved when they find his backpack stuffed in the corner of the auditorium, with all of his belongings still inside it.

The following Monday, there's an announcement about an assembly that will take place in the auditorium. All students are required to attend. The principal, some teachers, and the guidance counselor all talk about how the school needs to be a bully-free zone. That means students aren't allowed to fight, call people names, send rude emails or text messages to other students, or steal another student's belongings. All students, they say, should feel safe and cared for at school. The principal says that if any students see or hear of a bullying incident, they should report it immediately.

Diego feels better after that. He knows that if he's ever picked on again, he can go right to a teacher or the principal for help.

Later that day, after lunch, there's another surprise in Diego's locker. It's a handwritten note that says, "I'm sorry, Diego."

Asking for Help Isn't Tattling

Because of your ASD, you might find yourself in situations where other kids tease you, call you names, or pick on you in some way. Lots of kids who have ASD say that "typical" kids often don't treat them well. Have you been called names like "dummy," "loser," "freak," or something else? These names are meant to hurt your feelings and make you doubt yourself. Unfortunately, people sometimes make fun of what they don't understand. If you haven't been teased this way yet, it will probably happen sometime. It's part of life. A hard part!

Every kid is called names or bullied at one time or another. Sad but true! Why do people use hurtful names? Maybe they think being mean makes them more powerful. (It doesn't.) Keep in mind that their words aren't true. You're a great person who deserves respect—and that's what really matters.

If someone is bothering you, you can stick up for yourself by holding your head high (to show pride) and speaking with a firm voice. Being assertive like this shows you're willing to face the person, even if you feel scared inside. You can say things like "Back off," "Stop bothering me," or "I don't like what you're saying. Leave me alone." Another option is to ignore the person. Say nothing, turn your body away, or walk away.

Sometimes this is enough. Sometimes it's not. If you're being teased or treated poorly, get an adult's help. At school, you can tell your teacher, another teacher who's nearby, a recess monitor, the social worker or guidance counselor, the principal, the psychologist, your speech or OT teacher, or any other adult you recognize in the school building or on school grounds. It's helpful to let your parents or other grown-ups at home know what's going on too.

What if kids call you a "tattletale" or some other rude name because you've reported them? Try not to let it bother you too much. You haven't "tattled"—you've told an adult about a situation you need help with. The most important thing is for you to feel safe and supported.

Have you ever been bullied at school or in your neighborhood? Is there someone who targets you by saying mean things, pushing you around, taking your belongings, or making you do things that get other kids to laugh? Being bullied is scary and stressful. You might feel nervous, unhappy, lonely, or even helpless.

But you're *not* helpless. You *can* take a stand against someone who's bullying you. Here are 10 strategies that might work in your situation:

1. **Ignore the person who's bullying you.** Don't make eye contact, and pretend not to hear the person's words. Keep doing whatever it is you're doing: schoolwork, playing, talking to a friend.

2. **Try not to show emotion,** if possible. People who bully like to get a reaction. They want to see another person cry or get upset or angry. Even if you feel afraid and hurt, try to keep a calm expression on your face. You can talk about how you feel later, or you can write down the feelings to express them.

3. **Tell the person to leave you alone.** Do this in a straightforward way. Depending on the situation, you could say: "I don't like what you're saying," "That isn't true," "Leave me alone," or "Stop bothering me." Use a strong, firm voice. It's okay if other people overhear you. These people may be able to help if they realize you're being bullied.

4. **Walk away, quickly—or run.** Go to a place where there are more people so someone who bullies is less likely to keep bothering you. Find an adult and say exactly what happened. You can say, "I'm being bullied, and I need some help, please."

5. **Know that a true friend won't bully you.** If someone you consider a friend is doing the bullying, that's a particularly difficult situation. But a *true* friend wouldn't want to embarrass you or hurt your feelings. If a friend is making you do things you're not comfortable with, *stop*. Say "No," "I don't want to do this," or "I refuse to do what you're asking." Just because you've done it once or twice before doesn't mean you must keep doing it. You have the right to stop, and to make your own decisions.

6. **Let your family know about the problem *right away*.** Tell your parents so they can help protect you. Their job is to report

any bullying to the school. That way teachers and the principal become aware of what's going on. If you have older siblings at your school, you might want to tell them what's happening too. Then they can look out for you in the hallways, on the bus, and in other busy, crowded places.

7. **Get help from a trusted grown-up.** If your family isn't a strong source of support for you, find an adult you trust who can help you deal with the bullying problem. It's not your fault if you're being bullied. You deserve to feel safe at school, at home, and in your community.

8. **Surround yourself with people at school.** Walk through the hallways with friends, stick with your buddies at recess, and avoid being alone in the school bathrooms. (You might be able to get permission to use the bathroom in the nurse's office for a while, for example.) People who bully like to catch their targets when they're alone.

9. **Be aware of cyberbullying.** This takes place through internet or phone communication. People who bully online might make fun of someone in an app or post cruel messages online. They might send threatening emails or put up unflattering pictures of someone online. They might call another person's phone over and over, or send rude text messages. Only use the internet or a phone with a parent's permission. And be sure you know the rules about cyberspace safety. If you're bullied online or on the phone, tell an adult. Keep all the records for proof!

10. **Don't bring expensive or special belongings to school,** especially if another kid is taking your stuff. Label all your notebooks, jackets, and the soles of your shoes with your name, using permanent marker.

You know what else will protect you from bullying? And you know what can help you during those times when you're feeling lost and left out? FRIENDS. Friends are there for you in good times and bad. They help you out, make you laugh, and teach you how to get along with others. In Chapter 13, you'll learn about the importance of friendships. Keep using your Social Skills Survival Kit, and keep reading!

Making and Keeping Friends

Making friends is a lifelong skill—for anyone, whether the person has ASD or not. It's a skill you can start working on now, and one you'll continue to develop as you learn and grow. *Everyone* can improve their friendship skills—even adults. Talk to some grown-ups and you'll see! You'll probably hear that their friends still teach them about some of the most important things in life:

- sharing interests and activities
- spending time together
- connecting with others on a deeper level

Friends, in other words, are protection against loneliness. Do you get lonely sometimes? Maybe you're a person who enjoys spending time alone and has lots of cool hobbies. You still need other people. Humans are social creatures—even if they have problems with social skills! We all need to feel a connection with others. We need that feeling of being liked and accepted for who we are.

As a child, J.D. Kraus was diagnosed with Asperger's. In his book *The Aspie Teen's Survival Guide,* J.D. describes his experience of coming home after school on Fridays. There he would wait for his parents to get home from work: "I would . . . go to my room, close the door, and lie on my bed. I would stare at the ceiling and feel the isolation and loneliness build inside of me. There was no one to call, no one to hang out with. No one. Nothing." That changed when he found a friend in ninth grade. His new friend, another boy with ASD, helped J.D. experience the benefits of friendship. Together, they were no longer isolated and lonely.

What Is Friendship?

That may seem like an easy question . . . but it's more complicated than you think. Kids who have autism spectrum disorder don't always understand the difference between a *friend* and an *acquaintance.*

So, what *is* the difference, anyway?

An acquaintance is someone you see on a regular basis but may not know well. You might know the person's name and recognize their face. You might say hi to the person or make "small talk" by saying stuff like "How are you?" or "What's new?" Acquaintances may include: classmates, kids in higher and lower grades at school, neighbors, and teammates (if you're on a team). Kids who go to your place of worship, community center, or park are also acquaintances. So are adults you recognize—your parents' friends or people they work with, a librarian or coach, and neighbors.

An acquaintance is someone you might see almost every day or a few times a week. That person might be nice to you. That person might speak with you briefly, or even hang out with you for short periods of time. But it's usually not *friendship.* Friendship is bigger—and better.

A friend is someone you spend time with, doing things you both enjoy. There's a Spark, a connection that's meaningful and worth building on. The two of you might go to each other's homes. You might share a meal, see a movie, or play games. You might spend time talking and laughing face to face. You have something in common—like a hobby, an activity, or a collection. You like being together. Together, you have FUN.

The most important piece is *togetherness.* A friend wants to spend time with you. A friend will call you on the phone or invite you over. You'll spend time together in places other than school.

> I have a best friend. He has been kind to me and understands me. We've been friends since kindergarten. He doesn't have autism, but he doesn't care that I do.
>
> —14-year-old boy

Some kids who have ASD believe that classmates are the same as friends. But there's a difference. Even if you've known certain kids since kindergarten, you share a classroom, and you say hi each day, it's not necessarily *friendship.* But it could become a friendship! First, you've got to show people that you want to become friends. You might:

- Invite someone over after school.
- Send emails back and forth (if you have a computer or tablet and you're both allowed to use email).
- Join the same club or try out for a team together.
- Make a plan to see the person during the weekend—for example, at a park or movie theater.
- Ask your dad or mom for help making social plans with a kid you want to be friends with.

It helps to choose someone who's *likely* to be a friend. Think of someone who's usually nice to you, doesn't tease you, and seems to care about you in some way. Look for a person who shares your interests or talks to you at school. Someone who invites you to play at recess. Someone who asks you questions or seems open to being friends.

You might say, "I noticed you signed up for chess. I did too. Would you like to come to my house sometime for a game?" If the person says yes, then be ready to exchange phone numbers and set up a time to come over. Your mom or dad can help with that too.

> It takes a while for me to make new friends. You can't just run around and say to people, 'Hey, do you want to be my best friend?' They would think you're weird. If they talk to you a lot or wave to you or say hi, that means they might want to be your friend.
>
> —14-year-old boy

Why Is Making Friends Hard to Do?

Many kids struggle to find friends. They might not have strong social skills. They may be shy or get picked on. They may just feel more comfortable spending time alone. There are lots of different reasons why it can be difficult to make friends. But it's *so* important to try. Why? Because having friends leads to better health. People who have friends say they're happier and less stressed because they have people they can count on (other than family).

> Is there something I'd like to tell people who don't seem to understand me? Yes: I don't bite.
>
> —11-year-old boy

When you have ASD, "typical" kids may sense you're different in some way but may not know why. To them, you might seem a bit "odd" or somewhat of a loner. They may not realize you want to make friends. Or, they may have the (wrong) idea that you prefer to be left alone. If you've had any behavioral problems at school in the past, other kids might be a bit scared of you. Or they may not realize that, in some ways, you've grown. Many kids in your class or neighborhood may already have close friendships, and perhaps you've been left behind. Any of these situations may be true for you—but it's not too late! You can still make friends, and you can still learn to *be* a good friend. It's never too late for that.

Sometimes, no matter how hard you try, certain kids won't want to be your friend. It's not your fault. Find other kids and focus on them instead. Don't give up on making friends!

Being a Good Friend

Friendship means sharing more than interests and activities. It means sharing parts of *yourself.* You'll need to talk about your thoughts and feelings, even if it's hard to do, because that's key to friendship. Sometimes, you might share your knowledge or advice. Other times, you'll tell some of your secrets (like your most embarrassing moment or your dreams for the future). That's what friends are for.

Communication and conversation are big parts of friendship. You'll need those skills to be a good friend. If that seems scary, don't worry. All kids your age are learning those skills, not just kids with ASD, and not just you. You don't have to have perfect communication (no one does!) or be the world's greatest conversationalist. Do the best you can, knowing that your skills will improve over time.

Be open with your friends—let them know what you're working on. Here are some things you might say:

"I have a problem with interrupting, but I'm working on it. I hope you can be patient with me! If I interrupt while you're talking, you can let me know."

"Every once in a while, I say something that I wish I hadn't said. You can let me know if I ever hurt your feelings. Don't be afraid to tell me, because I might not figure it out on my own."

"Sometimes I talk too loud. Can you tell me if I do that?"

Liam's Story

Liam is in the fifth grade and has ASD. He knows the names of all the kids in his classroom and in other classes too. He loves to raise his hand to answer questions in class, because he's smart and he likes learning. He always sits next to someone during lunch at school. In gym class he's almost always picked for one of the teams for dodge ball. Liam thinks he has lots of friends and feels good in school.

But outside of school Liam doesn't have much of a social life. He hardly ever gets invited to someone's home to play, and he's never been asked to a sleepover. Liam doesn't understand why it's so hard for him to have friends to do stuff with after school. Sometimes he hears kids talking about a playdate or a birthday party, and Liam feels left out and sad because he wasn't invited.

Liam knows he has ASD, but he's not always sure just what it means. He gets good grades, and other kids are friendly to him—but Liam feels as if something is missing in his life. He decides to talk to his mom about the friendship problem.

Liam tells his mom that he's lonely and doesn't know if he's doing something wrong. His mom says that it's not his fault if friendship isn't easy for him. She tells him that friendship is challenging for many kids who are on the spectrum. But, she says, they can learn the social skills that will help them succeed. Liam feels better, especially when he and his mom come up with a Friendship Plan.

As part of the plan, Liam's mom calls Carl's mom. Carl and Liam have been at the same school since kindergarten, and they ride the same bus. Back in kindergarten, Liam went to Carl's birthday party and they had a few playdates. But that ended in first grade, when Carl found other friends in school and on his soccer team.

Liam's mom gets some helpful information from the phone call. Later on, she tells Liam that Carl admitted some of the other kids at school are a little afraid of Liam. Liam can hardly believe his ears! What could they be afraid of? His mom explains that the other students think of Liam as "the smartest boy in their grade." They like sitting with Liam at lunch.

But Carl said that sometimes Liam talks really loud. Then people think he's angry or upset. Also, some of the guys think Liam sits too close. They don't know how to ask him to move, so they try to avoid him instead.

Liam is confused by all he hears. He never realized he spoke too loud or sat too close to people. But he also knows he can change that. He likes it that the other kids think of him as smart, but he wants them to realize he's *more* than smart—he's friendly and fun too! He asks his mom what to do.

"Well," his mom says, "what would you think about telling the kids in your class about your ASD? Maybe that would help them understand you better."

Liam considers this. His classmates might tease him or think he's weird. On the other hand, being on the spectrum is a part of who he is. He decides that, with his mom's help, he can talk about ASD so other kids might better understand him. His mom tells him she will ask his teacher, Mr. Gilbert, to help Liam talk to the class.

Mr. Gilbert starts the presentation by saying, "All people are different. Everyone has strengths. Everyone has challenges. Today, Liam is going to tell you something about himself that you may not have known."

Suddenly, it's Liam's turn to talk. He's nervous, but he glances at his mom, who is smiling and looks proud. Liam takes a deep breath and imagines he's a teacher at the front of the classroom, explaining a lesson. He says: "I have something called ASD, or autism spectrum disorder. It means I have some problems with social skills." He goes on to describe his symptoms, such as talking too loud or not realizing when he's standing or sitting too close. He finishes by saying, "I don't mind if you ask me questions about ASD. And I really hope that some of you will be my friends."

Right away, kids raise their hands to ask questions. "How did you get ASD?" "What does it feel like?" "Is that why you're so smart?" Liam answers the questions as best he can, and sometimes his mom and Mr. Gilbert help with the answers too.

Then, to Liam's surprise, the kids clap. He sits down in his seat, feeling relieved—and happy. He knows he's something else besides smart: He's brave.

Like Liam, some kids who have ASD share that information with their classmates. This is a way to help others better understand how they act and communicate. It's up to you—and your family—to decide if that step is right for you. Some kids and families prefer to keep the diagnosis private, telling only relatives and very close friends. Talk to your parents or caregivers about the issue before deciding.

If you've made a friend, that's terrific! Now you'll probably need ideas for staying friends. A friendship is lots of fun, but it's also work. Staying connected takes effort. Here are some tips to try:

Be flexible. Do what your friend likes to do, even if it's not your favorite activity. Being flexible is important because otherwise your friend might feel as if you're making all the rules or decisions. Take turns choosing activities, and be a good sport by not complaining. For more on being a good sport, see pages 61–62.

Reach out. Even if you're not used to making phone calls or texting friends, you sometimes need to make the first move. Invite your friend to your home, plan a fun outing like going to the arcade, or have a sleepover.

Go places together. This helps create a stronger bond. Together, you'll have experiences out in the world, instead of only at home. Your outing doesn't have to be expensive. You could go to a free concert or museum, or try hiking or playing in a park. If you can spend a little money, head to a skating rink, an indoor play park, or a water park. See movies, go to sporting events, or volunteer together. If outings tend to be difficult for you, remember that your friend can support you and help make the experience more fun.

Show appreciation. Let your friend know you care. Do simple things: Make a birthday card or send a funny video. Give compliments. Help a friend with homework. Send your buddy a postcard if you're on vacation. Give your friend little gifts like a fun pencil or eraser or something you made yourself. You don't have to give presents often, but it's a thoughtful gesture when you do.

Be loyal and caring. If your friend gets a bad grade, say something kind, such as, "You seem upset. Is there anything I can do to help?" Show you care in other ways too. For example, stick up for your friends if they're being teased. Give friends a call at home when they're sick and can't go to school. Save a seat for a friend at the lunch table or on the bus, if you're allowed to. Leave a funny note at your friend's locker.

Take a Look!

Many of the skills you've read about in this book will help you make friends:

- Have you been working on getting along better with family members? (See Chapter 8.) *That* can help you get along better with kids your own age.

- Have you tried any of the ideas in Chapter 9—joining a club, starting a social skills group, or finding other kids who have similar hobbies? If so, the kids you're getting to know might become your friends.

- Are you practicing the listening skills from Chapter 10? Being a good listener is a key to friendship.

- The conversation tips from Chapter 11 can help you become more confident about talking with friends one-on-one and in groups.

- Finally, the Social Skill Survival Kit in Chapter 12 can help you build confidence in many social situations.

Kiko's Story

Kiko is 10 and very independent. Everyone always tells her dad how mature Kiko is for her age. They say she's "almost as responsible as an adult." Sometimes, people tell Kiko's dad: "She must be so popular."

Kiko is proud about the compliments. But she's also sort of sad, because the truth is she doesn't have many friends. In fact, she's not popular at all. Deep down, she knows popularity doesn't really matter—but she sure would like to have a couple of friends. Kiko's ASD makes it hard for her to be social in a way other people understand.

At school, the speech therapist helps Kiko practice her social skills. Kiko is learning appropriate ways to start conversations. She practices asking social questions. Kiko also works on listening, so she can be part of conversations at the lunch table and during recess. Kiko also practices in the cafeteria while eating lunch with the other girls. Things are going better. The other girls seem to notice her, and they don't drift away when she talks.

Today in the lunch line, Kiko decides to ask Megan a social question: "What do you like to eat?"

Megan says, "I like cookies. But my mom won't let me use any of the money from my lunch account to buy them. Can you believe that?"

This gives Kiko an idea. She puts a cookie on her lunch tray—not for herself but for Megan. Kiko knows this is *showing interest in what other people like,* something she's learned about in therapy. Then she goes to Megan's table and sits near her. "I got this for you, Megan," Kiko says, smiling.

"Thanks!" says Megan. Kiko can tell by the expression on her face that Megan is pleased.

The next day at lunch, Kiko buys two cookies with the money in her lunch account. She gives one to Megan and another to a girl named Janelle. After that, Megan and Janelle are extra nice to Kiko. They save her a seat at lunch and seem excited when she brings them more cookies. At home, Kiko tells her dad all about her two new friends.

For a month, Kiko keeps buying cookies for Megan and Janelle. They seem to like sitting with Kiko at lunch. For the first time in a long time, Kiko feels included.

But one day after school, Kiko's dad is waiting to talk to her. He says he got a notice from the school that all the money in her lunch account is gone. He's surprised, because he had paid enough for several months of lunches. That's when Kiko tells him that her new friends love to eat the cookies she buys them every day. "I have to buy the cookies, Dad," she explains. "Megan and Janelle expect it."

Kiko's dad tells her that real friends don't expect you to buy things for them. He says it's okay to buy treats or give little gifts once in a while, but it's not a rule or an expectation. And you don't do it all the time. "There's more to friendship than that," he says. "It's about having fun together, playing together, and helping each other out."

Now Kiko feels confused. Has she done something wrong? Is it possible that Megan and Janelle only like the cookies and don't really like Kiko herself? Will they still sit with her if she doesn't give them a treat each day? It's a lot to consider.

"Dad, what should I do?" Kiko asks.

He puts his arm around her shoulders. "I have an idea," he says. "What if you invite Megan and Janelle over this Friday after school. You can spend time together here, getting to know each other better."

Kiko agrees to the idea. Then she has a thought. "I know what we can do while they're here!" she says.

"What?" her dad asks.

"We'll bake cookies," Kiko replies, grinning. "I'll send Janelle and Megan home with a bunch of cookies, and they can bring them as snacks all week."

Friendships can be *forever.* Ask some of the adults in your life if they have friends they've known since childhood or their teen years. Chances are, they'll say yes. Maybe they've been close friends for 20 or 30 years—or longer! Keep working on your friendship skills so these relationships can grow as you grow. And so they can last and last.

Chapter 14

School Success

Many kids with ASD agree on this: School is harder for them than it is for most kids. There may be a struggle to learn or to fit in (or both). School is challenging because of all the "extras" that go along with it:

- crowded classrooms and hallways
- bells ringing, messages over loudspeakers, shouting at recess
- moving from subject to subject and place to place
- an expectation of neat work, even handwriting
- lunch and recess, where you're on your own to figure out what to do
- the need to listen continuously, even if listening is difficult
- feelings of confusion or not knowing what might come next
- assignments to keep track of and bring to and from school

No wonder school can be tough! Even if you love certain subjects and get good grades, some aspects of school may be hard to handle. At times, you might think it would be a lot easier if you could sit alone in a quiet room where you could learn in your own way and at your own pace. There'd be no extra demands. But unless you're homeschooled, that won't happen very often. In a school setting, being part of a *community* is at the heart of the learning process.

This has its ups and downs. On the downside, when you're in a building full of people, your sensory system (see Chapter 3) is under added stress. You might be bothered by bright lights, sudden noises, crowds, and having to stand in line. And when you're surrounded by kids all day, your social skills are tested again and again. You have to listen, talk, and interact, which raises your anxiety level. By the time you get home, you might feel exhausted. Or, you might be all wound up from stressful experiences in your school day.

But there *is* an upside. Besides learning, one of the positives of being in school is that you have daily opportunities to grow in areas that are difficult for you. Every day is a test of your communication skills and a chance to explore the social world. Every day is an opportunity to discover more about yourself, your needs, and how to get them met.

Take another look at pages 73–77, which focus on ways to get involved in special activities that help you learn and have fun. Many of these opportunities start at school: clubs, band, orchestra, school plays, sports, volunteering, and more. Activities like these can help extend your learning and increase your brain power—just a few more advantages of school.

Your IEP

IEP stands for Individualized Education Program. It's the written plan outlining the educational program and services that will meet your needs as a student. You need a special plan because you have a disability (ASD). Your ASD affects your ability to learn in school. A law passed in 1975, now called the Individuals with Disabilities Education Act (IDEA), helps make sure that *all* children, including those with a disability, have a right to a quality public education.

You may not think of yourself as disabled. Instead you might consider yourself "quirky" or "different" or "unique." You may be all those things! But it's still important to have an IEP. This plan helps the teachers and other adults at school understand you better.

As a student, you don't have to put together the IEP yourself. That's a job for your parents or caregivers and your school. There are steps that must be taken before an IEP is created, such as having a doctor or another expert let the school know about your diagnosis. Show this chapter to the adults at home so they can learn about IEPs or let you know if you have one in place.

You can be part of your IEP meetings, if you wish. Those meetings take place at school. They include your teacher, a special education teacher, and other experts who can support you.

An IEP includes many ways the people at school will help you, depending on your needs and what your parents, caregivers, and teachers request. Parents might request that their child:

- be able to sit near the teacher, and never have to change seats, even if the classroom is rearranged
- be allowed to take "sensory breaks" throughout the day, as needed, in a resource room or another place at school
- get extra time on tests
- receive special help in speech, social skills, or occupational therapy (OT) skills such as handwriting (if needed and approved)
- have a classroom aide to help with academics
- may call a parent during the school day, if needed, as a way to calm down or stay focused
- be allowed to use a special bathroom at school
- have extra classroom tools (such as a mini trampoline, an exercise ball to gently bounce on, a weighted vest or blanket, headphones, or communication tools)
- have a reward system in place, to encourage positive classroom behavior
- get extended deadlines on longer homework assignments
- have an additional set of textbooks at home, in case the child forgets them at school and needs to study or do homework

Each student's IEP is different. Yours might include some of the previous ideas, or other things. You can help with your IEP by letting the adults who teach and take care of you know more about your school experience:

- What's hard for you? What's easy for you?
- What do you like and dislike about school?
- Where might you need extra assistance?
- Is there anything that could help your days go more smoothly?

Keyan's Story

Keyan is in fourth grade, and because of his autism, he has sensory issues. Sometimes at school, he gets overwhelmed by all the noise, lights, and people. His IEP plan tells his teacher specific ways to help Keyan calm down and focus so he can learn better.

Keyan's teacher made a special space in the back of the classroom where Keyan can take breaks. Other students can use the space when they need time away too. This makes Keyan feel good. Something that helps him can help others as well!

Today in science, the students are doing an experiment with popping balloons. Keyan gets startled and bothered by loud noises. His teacher knows that Keyan may not want to participate. She tells him all about the experiment ahead of time. Then she asks if he'd like to wear his special sound-blocking headphones but still watch. Keyan decides he'd rather read about the experiment instead. Then, when the experiment takes place, he'll head to his quiet space at the back of the room.

When the time comes, Keyan goes to the back of the room. There, a bookshelf makes a divider. Behind the shelf, Keyan finds the giant beanbag chair he loves. He has a printout of the experiment to read. And there's music with headphones. As Keyan reads he listens to calm music that blocks out the rest of the classroom noise.

Before the school year and before your IEP is written, talk with your parents or members of your team of helpers (for more about this team, see Chapter 7) to come up with ideas for what might help you in the classroom and throughout the day. Your family and team members know you best—they can help make your IEP into a document that makes a difference in your school day.

Your family has opportunities to make changes to the IEP when something isn't working. A parent or caregiver can let the school know if it's time to meet about the IEP again. You and your family have a right to stand up for your needs. You don't have to wait!

Tools to Help You Get Organized

You might be one of those kids who has a clean locker, an organized backpack, and a nice, neat desk. Maybe you like rules and a sense of things being orderly—which helps you focus and feel safe. It's great that you're already focused on being organized. That will help you a lot in middle school and high school, where you have more classes, teachers, and schoolwork to keep track of.

Many kids on the autism spectrum don't have strong organizational skills, however. This is because of how their brains are wired. It's not a matter of intelligence—it's a matter of being weaker in the area of *executive function*. What does that mean? The executive function area of the brain helps a person plan and organize. It's like having a "personal assistant" inside your head, telling you how to stay on top of your day. Don't worry if your brain's "assistant" isn't so great at the job. Lots of tools can help you better focus, plan, and organize. They're right at your fingertips when you need them.

Handy-Dandy Planners

Using a daily planner can be the key to knowing what comes next. When you know what comes next, you feel more comfortable and confident. You'll be more likely to have what you need when you need it.

Kids with ASD do better when they have a daily schedule they can count on. Are you already using a visual schedule, a planner, or a calendar? If you're not, ask an adult at home to help you plan your days from morning until evening. Then you'll have a routine you can count on.

Page 142 shows a sample daily schedule for at-home use. Some families use a special planner or a dry-erase board. The schedule needs to be in a place where you can easily see it throughout the day. Check off each item as you finish—it feels great to accomplish your tasks!

For school, try a planner with one day per page so you'll have more room for all of your activities (see bottom of page 142). Write down all of your homework assignments and which materials to bring home. It's stressful when you forget to take home the books or folders you need or when you do your homework but forget to bring it back to school.

Wednesday

Morning:	☐	7:00	Alarm goes off, get dressed, get backpack and lunch ready
	☐	7:20	Breakfast
	☐	7:40	Wash face and brush teeth
	☐	7:45	Playtime until bus comes
	☐	8:00	Bus!
After School:	☐	3:30	Arrive home! Eat snack! Relax!
	☐	4:30	Piano lesson
	☐	5:00	Piano lesson ends—FREE TIME!
	☐	5:30	Do two chores from chore chart—then more FREE TIME!
Evening:	☐	6:00	Dinner (try one new food tonight)
	☐	7:00	Start homework (Dad will help)
	☐	8:00	Fun time with Mom
	☐	8:30	Start getting ready for bed
	☐	9:00	Bedtime, lights out!

Day of Week: Monday   **Date:** March 3

Assignment	Due
Reading Textbook pp. 140–150 — Bring book home!	tomorrow
Math Worksheet, pre-test handout — Bring math folder home!	tomorrow
English/Language Check out poetry book from library — Find library card!	by next Tuesday
Spelling Test Friday (study unit words) — List is at home	
Science No homework tonight—yay!	
Social Studies Work on report for 30 mins. tonight — Materials are at home	Friday

Teacher Message	Parent Message
Kira needs more graphing paper. —Mrs. M.	

Some kids with ASD have trouble working with paper planners or calendars or keeping track of little sticky-note reminders. Maybe the writing on them gets crowded and messy. Or the notes get crinkled or lost. If this is the case for you, you might want to use electronics to stay more organized.

Your family could set up an electronic calendar so you can all see each other's schedules at a glance. If you have access to a digital watch, phone, or tablet, you might use the Reminders or Notes functions to help you remember stuff you tend to forget. Typing entries into electronics may be simpler—and more fun—for you than writing by hand. Plus, electronic records last longer than sticky notes or to-do lists posted on the fridge. If you use a tablet at school, your teacher may be able to help you use an electronic planner for your schoolwork too.

"Neater Meter"

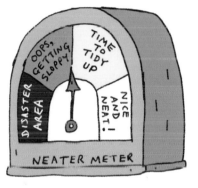

You may be disorganized and not even know it. Maybe you overlook the mess, or just become used to it. But having a sloppy desk, locker, or backpack slows you down. It's hard to find what you need, and the work you hand in to your teachers might be messier than it should be. Time to turn on your "Neater Meter"! Look at the areas around you.

You can start with your desk at school. What's inside it?

Take a peek in your locker. Is it a disaster, with old papers, rotten food, or out-of-season clothing in it (like a mitten from last winter)?

Now look inside your backpack. Take everything out of it and see what you've got. Are there several broken pencils at the bottom of it? How about bent, torn papers? Old snacks or used tissues?

Ask a parent or another trusted adult to help you clean out these different areas and get them in better shape. It's best to work with someone instead of trying to do this on your own. Cleaning up can be a long, difficult task. You may not know where to begin or how to keep going. Having a helper is motivating. That person can sort through your belongings and can also purchase any organizing supplies you may need, such as new folders or a pencil pouch.

Once you've tidied up, it's a matter of keeping your "Neater Meter" turned on and tuned in. How?

- **Locker.** Use the hooks and shelves provided to hang up your jacket and store extra shoes or boots. The top shelf can hold your books and notebooks. Never leave food in your locker, because it can rot.

- **Lunchbox.** Remember to bring your lunchbox home with you each day. Make sure you have your water bottle, containers, or utensils. At home, give the lunchbox to your dad or mom to clean and repack (unless you do those tasks yourself).

- **Desk.** At the end of each week, examine the inside of your desk. Are there papers you can take home? Do you need to sharpen your pencils or bring in new markers? Is the cap on your glue? Are your folders and notebooks stacked neatly? Is there food or candy that should be removed?

- **Subject folders.** Use color-coded folders for each subject. Write the name of each subject clearly on the front. Then place the folders in your backpack in subject order. (If you start the day with math, your math folder goes in first. If science is next, put the science folder behind the math one, and so on.)

- **Zippered pouch.** This can hold pencils, pens, erasers, a small ruler, highlighters, a glue stick, a calculator, tissues, and other items you need each day. With these things in one place, they won't get lost in your backpack or get smashed by your books.

- **Backpack.** Go through your backpack each night at home. Put your papers in the correct folders and toss any trash. After you do your homework, place your assignments and textbooks in the backpack so you won't forget them. Be sure to check your daily planner one last time to see if you've finished all your work.

- **Gym bag.** If you have a gym bag or sports bag, be sure to regularly clean that out too. Remove the dirty clothes for washing. Give your shoes a chance to air out. Wash the water bottles. Place everything back in the bag before your next practice.

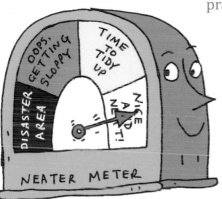

Being neat and tidy can become a good habit. You'll probably discover that having a clean desk, backpack, and locker makes it easier for you to find your belongings and homework and keep track of them. All of this can add up to higher grades and increased confidence. Keep trying—it's worth it! Ask for help anytime you start to feel as if the needle on your "Neater Meter" is pointing to the sloppy side.

Homework Habits

Homework is a "have to." It's not fun, but you have to get it done! To make sure your homework time is efficient, set up a routine you can count on:

- Work at a desk or table in a quiet place—a *homework station*. Use a bright lamp so you can see well.
- Gather all the materials you'll need so you don't have to stop your work to go find markers, a pencil sharpener, glue, etc.

- Eat a healthy snack like a piece of fruit so you won't get hungry. Keep a water bottle nearby to sip from.
- Do the hardest work first to get it done while you're still energized. (Later in the evening, you'll probably be more tired.)
- Focus on using neat handwriting and the correct pencil grip—it's frustrating sometimes, but you can do it!
- Set a timer for breaks. Maybe you need to get up and stretch every 15 minutes.
- Ask a parent or another grown-up to check over your work once you've finished. Make any needed corrections. Then put your homework back in the correct folders. Put all your folders and books in the backpack, zip it up, and you're done!

"Unstructured" Times at School

Most of the school day is *structured,* meaning there's a schedule of tasks and activities to complete. For example, you have math class, where your teacher may stand at the front of the room and go over the lesson. Students are expected to listen and learn the material. This is true for many classes throughout the school day, even gym. In gym class, you may play a game or do a workout. But there are still rules, and an adult who watches to be sure kids are doing what they're supposed to do.

What about the unstructured times like when you're walking through the hallways? Or recess and lunch? Many kids with ASD say the *unstructured* parts of the day are the most difficult for them. It may seem as if lunch should be easy. All you have to do is eat, right? And it may seem as if recess is pure fun—all that shouting and running around. But for kids with ASD, these times are loud, crowded, and confusing. There aren't clear rules they can count on. Things change all the time: where kids sit, what they talk about, who they hang out with, and what games they play.

If lunch, hallway time, and recess are difficult for you, you can let the adults at school and at home know this. Maybe you've felt stressed during these parts of the day, but didn't know why. Or maybe you never realized things could change for the better. But they *can*—there are lots of ideas to try.

Hallways

- Ask to have your IEP state that you're allowed to leave the room five minutes before the other students are excused to go to the next class or activity. This gives you extra time to get where you need to go while the halls are quieter.

- What if you don't want to walk alone or have trouble finding your way around the building? Ask to have an aide, a teacher, or another student accompany you each time.

- Keep a set of ear plugs in your pocket or desk. Put them in before hallway time to block out some of the noise.

- To further block out sounds and commotion, recite some kind of memorized list in your mind: the multiplication tables, the states or provinces in alphabetical order, or whatever you'd like.

Recess

- Try to join a game like tag, four square, hide and seek, or chase. This is an easy way to be social and have a structure—a game with rules!

- Swing to calm yourself down. Or, have fun on the slide. The rhythm of waiting for your turn, climbing up, and sliding down can feel familiar and soothing.

- Avoid being alone. It's stressful to wander around the playground, not knowing what to do or who to hang out with. Is there at least one friend you can count on? Make plans with that person ahead of time. Say something like, "Want to play with me at recess?" Stick together!

- Ask for a recess buddy. If making friends is difficult for you and you need some help with social skills, a recess buddy is a great option. This student gets the special responsibility of helping you at recess. You can play together, join in a game, or practice conversation. Your mom or dad can help arrange for this.

- Bring something special to play with at recess: trading cards, a toy, or a ball, for example. (Get permission first.) This way, you can invite other kids to share the item with you. Instant fun!

- Some days, you might need to skip recess. It's true that recess is a great opportunity for exercise. Still, there may be days you need time alone between classes to settle down and de-stress. Find out if there's a place in school where you can go on days when recess is too hard for you.

Jordan's Story

Recess is fun, but boy can it get crazy, thinks Jordan, a third grader. All the screaming and running around gets on his nerves. He has tried wearing ear plugs, but they fall out when he hangs from the monkey bars or zooms down the slide. Jordan's autism makes it harder for him to join other kids in their games. He likes calmer activities. It's frustrating that the other kids seem to know just what to do. Some of them run right to the jungle gym. Others quickly start a game of Freeze Tag. A few hang around the edges of the playground to talk. By the time Jordan gets up the courage to join in, it's time to go to lunch.

Today Jordan's class is having indoor recess because it's raining. All the students will go to the Multipurpose Room. Jordan thinks it will be noisy, and he isn't looking forward to it. Then he remembers his marble collection in his backpack. He'd brought it in for Sharing Time to show his class.

Jordan loves his marbles. Some of them were given to him by his grandfather, from the days when he was a boy. They're all the colors of the rainbow. He loves how they sound when they roll and click together.

Jordan decides to ask his teacher if he can bring the marbles to indoor recess to play with. She says it's fine. *Cool,* Jordan thinks. *Now I have something to do!* He goes to a quiet corner to play to make sure the marbles won't roll away and get lost.

Jordan is having so much fun shooting marbles that he doesn't notice the crowd of kids gathered around him. One of them asks, "Hey, Jordan, can we play too?"

Jordan can't believe it. Usually, *he's* the one who has to ask others to play. Jordan shows the students his collection and teaches them different marble games. "Maybe you can start your own marble collections," he tells them. Jordan hopes that some of them will. Then they could trade marbles and learn more marble games together.

When it's time for lunch, the kids help Jordan clean up the marbles. "Thanks for playing, Jordan," they say.

"Any time!" he says. And he means it.

Lunchtime

- If waiting in the cafeteria line is difficult for you, bring your lunch every day or a few times per week.
- If noise is a problem, sit at a table where students are quieter.
- Think of a subject to talk about. Then use lunchtime to practice your conversation skills. (Read Chapter 11 for more on this.)
- If talking is difficult, start with simply listening. Make some eye contact, nod your head when appropriate, or laugh along with others. (See Chapter 10 for more on listening.)
- Invite a parent to join you at lunch once in a while. It's a good chance to spend time together.

Making the Most of School

At school, you have so many people you can go to for further assistance. If you're in special education, your teacher is trained to help you in subjects you struggle with *and* to come up with ideas for improved behavior and social skills. You may spend part of the day in a resource room where you get extra help and a break from larger classrooms. You may also work with an occupational therapist or a speech therapist at school. The school counselor or social worker is trained to help you too.

Any time you're facing tough challenges at school, talk to your mom or dad, your teachers, your principal, or your aide (if you have one). They will probably have good ideas for making the most of school. You may need a tutor in certain subjects, or to take special tests designed to help experts figure out your unique learning style. It's important to explore options so you can find what helps you succeed.

But YOU play a big role in your own success too! How? Try hard in all your subjects. Do your homework, and make sure your work is neat and correct. Whenever something isn't working well for you at school, speak up. Changes can be made to your IEP. It's an important tool for helping you get the most out of your school experience.

School teaches you not only about academics but also about getting along in a community of your peers. Your school can be a place to discover your talents, make friends, and learn. All that learning makes you smarter, stronger, and more prepared for the future. Think of school as a *positive* in your life—even if your days are sometimes difficult because of the social demands you face. You're a special kid with a lot of potential and so much ahead of you in life. Always believe in yourself!

Chapter 15

Tech Talk

Personal technology: it's everywhere. Smartphones, tablets, gaming systems, computers . . . the list goes on. You've probably been using electronics since you were a little kid. And you might love them. Really, *really* love them. People on the autism spectrum tend to have particular interests they grow passionate about, hoping to become experts, wanting to spend most of their time on that one thing. Maybe you feel that way about gaming? Or watching certain movies over and over?

There are advantages to having technology as a part of your life. You may use a tablet or laptop for your schoolwork. You may do research online. You may stay in touch with friends and relatives through video chatting and social media. If you're nonverbal or have difficulty with language, you may use technology to communicate in words or symbols. Or, if you have challenges with identifying facial expressions or emotions, there are certain apps that can help you with that. Technology is a helper. It can connect you to people and information. It lets you learn and relax.

So, what's the problem? Isn't technology simply *great*? Yes, but no. For some kids and teens on the autism spectrum, problems start with "overuse." (Too much of a good thing isn't *always* a good thing.) Young people who get too much tech time may face tough consequences: problems with behavior, social skills, learning, emotions, and physical fitness.

Let's be honest: as a person with ASD, you're already dealing with struggles in some of those areas. So the adults in your life probably have concerns about how much technology use is too much for you. They want you stay safe and healthy. They'd like to see your behavior improving over time. And you? You probably just want to have fun and get the chance to do what your friends and other kids do.

Shanti's Story

Shanti, who's nearly 13, is used to her autism by now. She knows about her strengths and the things she still needs to work on. But at times, she just wants to feel like everyone else. As her birthday nears, Shanti is excited about her mom's promise to get her a smartphone. She has already picked out the phone and a beautiful phone case with pictures of pink horses on it.

On the big day, Shanti's mom talks about the rules Shanti will need to follow when using her new phone. Rule 1: Shanti can't have the phone in the morning while getting ready for school—too distracting. Rule 2: She's not allowed to use the phone at school. Rule 3: As soon as Mom gets home from work, Shanti must give the phone to her because nights are for homework and family time.

"WHAT?!"

All the other kids Shanti knows can have their phones whenever they want.

Shanti decides to make the best of the situation. For several hours after school each day, she uses her phone to go online and chat with her friends. At first, everything goes well. Shanti is so excited to have her own phone, she almost doesn't mind handing it over to Mom when she gets home. But soon Shanti starts to feel frustrated when she can't have her phone back even after she has finished her homework and there are still hours before bed. She wonders what her friends are posting and chatting about together. What's she missing?

Soon the "phone fights" start. Whenever Shanti's mom asks for the phone, Shanti argues or begs for more time. Her mom has to pull the phone out of Shanti's hands. Then Mom gets the idea to hide the phone from Shanti at night. Shanti sneaks out of her room after everyone's asleep to find the hiding spot. Then she checks her social media late into the night, and remembers to put the phone back in its place.

So what if she's grouchy in the morning? Or tired all day at school? Shanti finally feels like a typical teenager, like she's fitting in. Then one day at school, Shanti falls asleep in class. The teacher notifies the school counselor, who then calls Shanti's mom.

Oh, boy. Shanti and her mom have a *huge* fight. Shanti has to admit she's been staying up too late. She confesses to using her phone after hours. Her mom tells her she needs to "learn self-control." Well, learning self-control is hard for any teen, but especially one with autism.

Mom and Shanti aren't sure how to work out this conflict. So they go to the school counselor for some advice. The counselor suggests that, instead of taking the phone away, Shanti's mom could allow her to earn extra phone time after completing her other activities. If Shanti does *all* her homework after school, she can have her phone for 30 minutes. After dinner, Shanti can do a few chores to earn more phone time. Mom can even offer the phone as a surprise reward when Shanti's behavior is really good. Still, that phone has to "go to bed" every night! And stay there.

Shanti and her mom follow this technology plan, and life at home improves. Shanti no longer feels tired from staying up way too late. She's working on being more responsible, and her mom likes the changes taking place. Shanti is so proud of herself that she decides to do a project at school about how teens can better manage their phone use. The project earns Shanti an "A." And, surprise! Her mom decides to reward her—with some extra phone time.

What the Doctor Says

Elizabeth Reeve, one of the authors of this book, is a doctor. She works with a lot of kids who have special needs, in particular those on the autism spectrum. Often, families come to Dr. Reeve with the same types of questions about the "proper" and safe use of technology. Parents wonder: *How much screen time is appropriate? Why does my kid get "so obsessed" with tech? Is it dangerous for my child to be online? Help!* Kids want to know: *Why are there so many limits? What's the big deal? Why can't I just do what I want!?*

Here's the scoop: we all use tech. Technology teaches, entertains, and connects people around the world. It's an important part of our lives. Just like "typical" kids and teens, young people on the spectrum need the opportunity to learn to be safe and healthy while using devices. But for kids with ASD, there can also be some special challenges.

Balancing time and energy. It can be easy to get super involved in gaming or chatting. This is especially true for some kids on the autism spectrum. Before you know it, hours have passed, and you're still focused on that screen. Other important things—like friends, family, homework, and outdoor activity—can lose out.

Making the switch. The time when you switch from one activity to another is called a *transition*. Switching the screen to "off" can be a real challenge and can lead to constant conflicts.

Staying safe online. This is an issue for anyone who goes online. It's especially important for kids with ASD. Why? Because their tendency to get super focused and explore deeply can lead them to unsafe sites. How can you stay away from inappropriate websites and not get in trouble on social media? What if you experience *cyberbullying*—bullying that takes place over phones, tablets, and computers?

Every family has to figure out how to use technology in their lives. There aren't any "one-size-fits-all" answers. Dr. Reeve tells families that it's helpful to create a set of rules and expectations spelled out for *everyone* in the family—not just for the child with autism. How? By setting up a Family Media Plan, based on what the American Academy of Pediatrics (AAP) recommends.

You can find the AAP family media guidelines at HealthyChildren.org /MediaUsePlan.

Your plan can address the kinds of technology and media that your family uses. It can help you set limits on the hours per day spent with electronic devices, based on each person's age. When a limit is set and followed, those transitions off a device are less tense. The plan can also set up practices that can keep you and your family safe online.

Do you wish your family would never see such a plan so you can hide in the corner with your phone forever? Nah, a spider could end up building a web on you! It's good to have a clear plan that adds structure to your daily life. You can print out or write and illustrate the plan you and your family create together and hang it in a common area of the home. That way everyone can see the plan and know what to do.

Some Screen Time Do's and Don'ts

DO get approval from parents on which shows, video games, computer games, and websites are allowed.

DO accept that "parental controls" may be placed on electronic devices.

DO make sure your chores, homework, and other responsibilities are finished *before* starting your screen time.

DO include family adults and siblings in your screen use, when appropriate. This way, you spend more family time together while getting to do the thing you like to do.

DO use electronic devices in common areas of your home (not closed off in a room by yourself).

DO break up your screen time into 20-minute or 30-minute segments. Why? Because these "stops" and "starts" will help you practice transitions! Kids with ASD often find transitions from one event to the next to be annoying or frustrating. When you rehearse leaving behind one (loved) activity for another (not-so-loved) activity, you're learning a skill. You practice patience. You take little steps in handling uncomfortable emotions. And that's a big win.

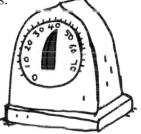

DO set up a timer or create a five-minute warning system when you're using electronics so you know when it will be time for you to stop.

DO keep electronics out of the bedroom at night. (It's too tempting to get up and use them.) If you need music to fall asleep, use a music player that doesn't have internet access. Get a plug-in or battery-powered alarm clock instead of using a phone to wake you up.

DO let parents monitor your texts, social media, and website use. It's important that they can check to be sure your online activity is safe.

Don't use passcodes that can lock parents out of devices.

Don't download new games or make in-app purchases without first getting your parents' okay.

Don't use electronics in the morning while getting ready for school. Mornings can be difficult for kids with ASD. Screens add more distraction. It may be helpful to allow yourself 10 minutes of screen time *after* you're fully ready for school—as a motivator. But only if you've become good at putting the screen away when your time is up!

Don't use screens for an hour before bedtime because they energize your brain and can keep you awake.

Don't rely on electronics as your *only* entertainment when spending time with friends. Go outside, play board games, have fun with crafts, or think of other fun activities to do.

Don't share passwords or personal information with people outside your family. (See more about this on page 158.)

Don't use electronics during meals. This is especially important if you have ASD because mealtime is a chance to practice social skills with no distractions. Mealtime is also for focusing on learning to try new foods. (Not just for you—for all family members.)

Don't let your electronics get gross: regularly wipe off fingerprints, dust, and grime. (Take a look at Chapter 23 about hygiene. It's good to "keep it clean.")

Ryder's Story

Ryder is a sixth grader with ASD. When he gets together with his friends, they like to play video games best of all. Sometimes, they gather in person. Other times, they all play the same game online from their own homes. They wear headphones and communicate through the game.

Ryder enjoys the video games—*a lot*. It's fun to have friends who are all into the same activity. And it's awesome to be able to talk and play without even leaving the house! Sometimes, Ryder just likes to be alone on his game controller with no one else in the room and yet still be social.

Ryder's parents want him to do more "face-to-face" get-togethers and less gaming. They say, "It's important for you to be with 'real people.'" *I am doing things with real people,* thinks Ryder. *So what if it's on screens?* These days, nearly everyone Ryder knows uses social media. Lots of kids text, post, and talk online. Why shouldn't *he?* Just when Ryder thinks he's getting through to his parents on using technology, something goes wrong. Very wrong.

One rainy day, Ryder and his friends are all stuck indoors and can't get together. They play their favorite online game for hours. Things get . . . competitive. One friend says Ryder isn't following the rules. Another one says Ryder cheated—but he *didn't*! Ryder tries to defend himself. That's not easy to do, because having autism makes communication harder. Ryder can't seem to get the words out. No one takes his side.

A few of the guys say Ryder should leave the game. For days, they get stuck on the idea that he's a cheater. At school, they don't act friendly like they usually do. When Ryder finally finds the courage to text his friends asking if he can rejoin the online game, they don't respond. Ryder feels angry, sad, and ignored.

When Ryder tries to get advice from his parents, they don't seem to understand. They're just happy to hear he won't be gaming as much. That's when he makes a mistake. Ryder posts a threatening message to his friends online. The next day at school, he's called into a meeting with the principal and his parents. Ryder tries to explain: "All I wanted was for my friends to know how angry I felt." But he knows he was wrong, and he's ready to apologize.

The school helps set up a plan for Ryder and his friends to talk about what happened. Then the school counselor gives Ryder and his friends information about using social media in responsible ways. Now, if Ryder's friends ever text or post something that confuses him, he knows to go to his parents for help. They're trying to be more understanding about Ryder's technology use. Every so often, they look at his phone and computer messages to make sure Ryder is communicating well. Ryder feels okay about this because he wants everyone to trust him. And, thanks to Ryder, his friends also learned a lesson about communicating in healthy ways instead of ignoring someone.

You've probably been learning in school about being a good digital citizen. Good digital citizenship is about media literacy (understanding what you learn or create) and staying safe and respectful online. You don't have to wait until the school explains it all, though. You can start now, at home, by following a few digital safety tips:

5 Tips for Good Digital Citizenship

1. Keep your personal information *private*—when you're online, never share things like passwords, your home address, or which school you attend. Only share photos with permission from your parent.

2. Respect other people's privacy online. For example, don't share their personal photos without asking first. Don't forward texts without permission.

3. Use kind words when online (and always!). Take care not to be rude. Don't make hurtful comments or threats. If you say something that bothers someone, apologize and try to make things right.

4. Tell a parent if you see things online that make you feel uncomfortable. Talk together openly about privacy and what is or isn't appropriate. If you receive any confusing or scary texts, messages, or photos, tell an adult you trust.

5. Let a parent or another adult know if you're being cyberbullied. Have you received rude texts or inappropriate photos? Have you been called names or teased online? Is someone using hurtful words through an online gaming platform or chat room? If any of this happens, show an adult what's going on.

Balance Is the Key

So you love your electronics—fine! You still need BALANCE, though. Make sure you get at least one hour of physical activity each day, plus lots of outdoor, fresh-air, screen-free time to stay healthy. If exercise isn't one of your favorite activities, then use your electronics for inspiration. For example, you and a parent may decide it's okay to use a screen to entertain yourself while riding an exercise bike or running in place. It's also important—in terms of balance—to watch what you eat and how much sleep you get each night. Read on to learn more about all of these "Body and Brain Basics," starting in Part 3.

Part 3

Body and Brain Basics

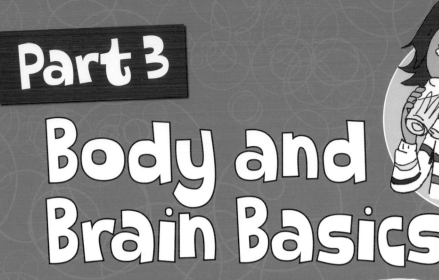

Chapter 16

How to Handle Hard-to-Handle Feelings

People who have ASD often describe themselves as very logical. That's a great asset! Using logic can help you make sense of situations and figure out what might happen next. You're most likely a fact-lover too—someone with a great memory for information and trivia. But when it comes to understanding and expressing emotions, that's probably a challenge for you.

Everyone has strong feelings at times. But when you have ASD, you tend to have a lot of intense emotions that come on suddenly. Your feelings may be hard for you to handle, especially if you also have sensory issues like those described in Chapter 3.

What does this mean for you? Well, it might seem like you have more bad days than good ones. Or there may be times during the day when you feel like you just can't handle the stress. That can add to the tension you're already experiencing. Stress often leads to an increase in those hard-to-handle feelings. And so it goes, around and around, as if you're caught in a circle:

To top it off, you probably find it hard to communicate what's bothering you. For example, if someone bugs you at school, you might not know what to say right at the moment to make the person stop. Or maybe you dislike riding the bus because of all the movement and sounds. Your reaction might be to get frustrated and "shut down." At home, you might feel angry about the amount of homework or chores you have, which can lead to a feeling of . . . ACKKK! When you feel like that, you might want to yell or be by yourself. It's sometimes difficult to say, "Help me, I'm stressed." But asking for help is the key to getting a handle on those hard-to-handle feelings.

What's the Problem?

Something a lot of people with ASD have in common is that emotions can be like a puzzle to them. This is true for their own feelings and other people's too. For example, studies have shown that people on the autism spectrum don't look at the human face in the same way that a "typical" person does. They look not at the *eyes* but at the mouth or nose.

Eyes give us a lot of information. They've been described as windows into what a person is thinking and feeling. If you're not looking in the window, you might miss important clues about another person's emotions. Sometimes, what someone *says* doesn't match what the person really *feels.* But you wouldn't necessarily know that unless you were looking the person in the eye and "reading" the emotions.

You can find out more about "reading" other people's thoughts and feelings in Chapters 10 and 11. Before you take on the challenge of trying to understand other people's emotions, a great goal is learning to recognize and understand your *own.*

How to Identify Your Emotions

How do you start to identify your feelings? There are signs that give you clues to what you are feeling.

Signs That You're Feeling Good

Good is a general term. It's a word most people use in everyday language to express that they're "okay" or not feeling "bad." So *good* can mean you feel any of these ways:

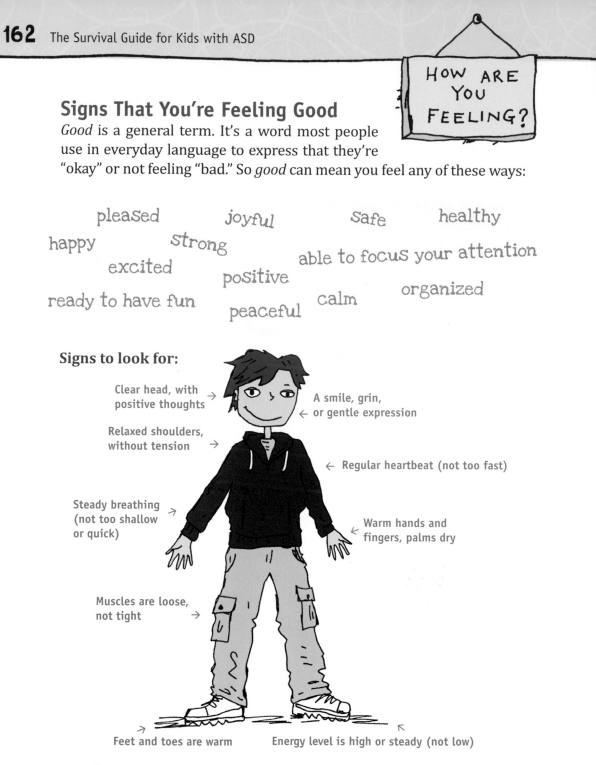

pleased   joyful   safe   healthy

happy   strong   able to focus your attention

excited   positive   organized

ready to have fun   peaceful   calm

HOW ARE YOU FEELING?

Signs to look for:

Clear head, with positive thoughts →

← A smile, grin, or gentle expression

Relaxed shoulders, without tension →

← Regular heartbeat (not too fast)

Steady breathing (not too shallow or quick) →

← Warm hands and fingers, palms dry

Muscles are loose, not tight →

→ Feet and toes are warm   ← Energy level is high or steady (not low)

When you feel this way, you're *balanced.* You're ready to learn. You're able to listen and follow through. You feel friendlier and more relaxed. Being balanced feels . . . good.

Signs That You're Feeling "Bad"

Bad is another one of those all-purpose terms—in this case one that people use to describe negative feelings. Feeling "bad" doesn't mean you're a "bad person." And it doesn't mean it's *bad* to feel "bad." Confusing, right?

When you're feeling *bad,* you might feel some of these ways:

worried   unhappy   down   angry

sad   scared   stressed out   alone   frustrated

sick   disorganized   upset

panicky   anxious   freaked out   confused

overloaded

Signs to look for:

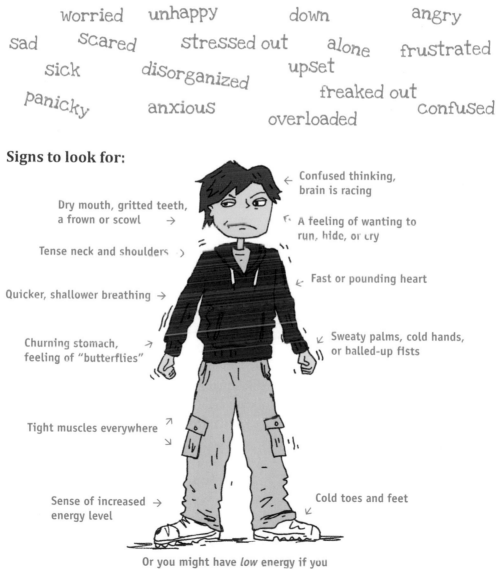

← Confused thinking, brain is racing

Dry mouth, gritted teeth, a frown or scowl →

← A feeling of wanting to run, hide, or cry

Tense neck and shoulders →

Quicker, shallower breathing →

← Fast or pounding heart

Churning stomach, feeling of "butterflies" →

← Sweaty palms, cold hands, or balled-up fists

Tight muscles everywhere ↗

Sense of increased → energy level

Cold toes and feet ↙

Or you might have *low* energy if you feel sad, down, and lonely.

These physical and emotional symptoms are signs that you're feel-ing *out of balance.* Your body fills with adrenaline—energy-boosting chemicals that make you feel like running, hiding, or even hitting. In a flash, you might feel out of control. This can lead to a meltdown.

Sometimes, young people with ASD have meltdowns because the strength of their emotions is confusing and upsetting. Do you often (or sometimes) get so angry or stressed out that you:

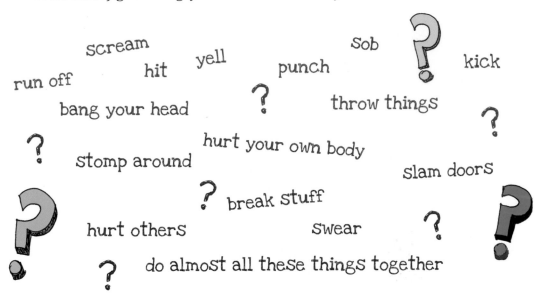

scream   hit   yell   punch   Sob   kick   run off   bang your head   throw things   hurt your own body   stomp around   slam doors   break stuff   hurt others   Swear   do almost all these things together

Meltdowns are really tough—on *everyone!* When you *feel* out of control and *get* out of control, it's scary. You might briefly feel a sense of power when you're melting down. But you're probably left with nega-tive feelings afterward—like sadness, regret, and confusion. You might worry that a punishment will follow. That never feels good.

When you're in the middle of a meltdown, one of the last things on your mind is what *other* people are feeling. But the truth is, they're probably getting frustrated with you or angry, upset, and hurt.

If you're at school, a big, angry outburst or meltdown puts nega-tive attention on you. Other students might say something not-so-nice to you later. You might feel embarrassed afterward. In some cases, other kids might even try to get you mad again, just to see if you have another outburst.

At home, your family probably has a hard time handling your melt-downs too. Your parents and siblings get upset when you're upset. Often, they're the ones who have to clean up if you've damaged stuff in anger. Nobody feels better after a meltdown. Not even you.

Guess what? You can learn to stop a meltdown before it starts. It takes some work and some practice—but it's worth it. There are *lots* of healthy ways to handle feelings.

How do you begin? You can start by doing your own "emotions self-check." At different points during an average day, take a moment to ask yourself how you feel. Notice your breathing, your heartbeat, your body temperature. Are you calm? Focused? Alert? Good!

Look around. *Who* are you with when you feel positive and content? *What* activity helps you feel this way? *Where* do you feel good? (At home, at school, in an after-school club?) *When* do you feel good? (Certain times of day or night?) *Why* do you feel good? Is it something you're doing—and can do *more* of?

Or, are you getting a bit stressed and worried? Does your body feel unbalanced? Is there something on your mind?

Again, ask yourself the *who, what, where, when,* and *why* of it. Pay attention to the situations that lead to stress or other difficulties.

If you're feeling bad at any given time, it's okay. Take a deep breath and get ready to use some tools from your toolbox.

Your Tools for Handling Emotions

Four tools can help you as you work to understand and handle your feelings. They aren't tools like a hammer and nails. Instead, they're an imaginary set of tools you can picture in your mind. Each tool can be used to take care of yourself when you're getting upset or experiencing intense emotions you need to get a handle on.

Tool #1: Oxygen

As soon as you start to feel "bad" or off-balance, close your eyes and your mouth and take a deeeeep breath through your nose. Shallow breaths go only as far as your chest. Deep breaths go down to your belly. Your stomach should rise as you inhale. Now exhale through your mouth. Do it again, and again. Getting oxygen to your brain helps you think more clearly. (See Chapter 19 for more breathing exercises.)

Tool #2: Antenna

You don't have an antenna growing out of your head, giving you information about yourself and your environment. (But it sure could come in handy.) Often, having ASD means you aren't "in tune" with yourself and what's going on around you. This can lead to that off-balance feeling mentioned earlier.

Sometimes, it's the simplest things that can help when something doesn't feel right. Tune in by asking yourself some basic questions: *Am I thirsty? Hungry? Overtired? Do I need to use the bathroom?*

Take a Look!

This chapter has tools to help you figure out HOW you feel, WHY you feel that way, and how to help yourself cope with intense feelings. It would be nice if you could read the chapter and then—*presto!*—be an expert on emotions for the rest of your life. But it doesn't work like that. Learning to understand your feelings takes time and practice. In fact, many people work on this *all their lives,* whether they have ASD or not. As human beings, we're emotional creatures, even if we're capable of logic. We have a lot of feelings that leave us confused and uncertain where to turn.

Learning to understand your feelings and express them is a skill to work on now—and forever! The more you do it, the easier it gets.

Make sure to keep yourself hydrated by drinking water throughout the day. Eat a healthy snack between meals. Get the rest you need. When you feel the urge to go to the bathroom, try to notice it right away—don't wait until the very last minute. Remembering to take care of your body helps you feel more balanced—physically *and* emotionally.

Tool #3: Walkie-Talkie

One of the best things you can do when you're off-balance, stressed out, or upset is to *communicate* these feelings. Walk over and talk to someone! Go to a parent, a teacher, or another adult you trust. Sometimes, the words don't come easily, so memorize a few phrases you can say:

- "I'm upset. Can you help me?"
- "I'm having feelings I don't know how to handle."
- "I need to talk to you about something."

Cry if you need to. Get the feelings out by talking about them. Listen to the adult too. This person might be able to help you solve the problem. The adult might also find a place for you to calm down.

Remember to try *talking it out* instead of *acting out*. (Acting out is doing something with your body instead of your words—things like hitting, kicking, punching, destroying property, or hurting yourself.) Let your feelings be known so other people can help you.

> Now that I am older, I can better express myself when things are vexing me. There are still times when I am bottled up like a clam, but talking to someone about my troubles has been good medicine for relieving my stress.
>
> —J.D. Kraus, from his book *The Aspie Teen's Survival Guide: Candid Advice for Teens, Tweens, and Parents from a Young Man with Asperger's Syndrome*

Note for Adults

ASD makes it very difficult for children and teens to manage their feelings when they're angry, upset, or melting down. Challenging as this is for you, the calmer *you* are, the easier you make it for your child to gradually calm down. Stay quiet and patient; guide your child to breathe deeply. Calming down after any kind of upset can take a while, for your child and you. See Chapter 19 for tips on creating a Calm-Down Space at home.

Tool #4: Rubber Band

Picture a rubber band. What's it like? *Rubbery, stretchy, flexible.* You can twist it and bend it in many directions, but a rubber band still goes back to its original shape without breaking.

What does this have to do with you? Like a rubber band, you can become more flexible.

Part of having ASD is *liking things a certain way.* Maybe you fear change. Maybe you feel safer when you know what to expect each day. For example, perhaps you eat only certain foods. Or maybe you have a hard time at school when the unexpected happens, like you get a substitute teacher one day. You may be afraid to try new things because something new feels scary or threatening to you—even if the new thing is something fun, like a movie or a different restaurant.

All of these are signs of *rigid thinking*—of being less flexible than you could be. When something happens that you don't like or didn't expect, you might suddenly feel "bad." (The physical symptoms mentioned on page 163 are signs to look for.) You get frustrated and angry more quickly, because you're locked into a certain way of thinking. That's known as *rigidity.*

But you can learn to be flexible. You probably know that you can make your body more flexible by bending and stretching your muscles. You can also become more flexible in your thinking. Using your "rubber band" tool (thinking of yourself as willing to bend), you can make little changes in your thinking. Over time, these small changes can make a BIG difference in how you feel.

At times when something isn't going the way you want, bend your mind a tiny bit. Take a deep breath first. Try not to react or act out. Instead, tell yourself:

- "It's okay. I can find a way to solve this problem."
- "I can try, even though I'm scared."
- "People will help me. I can go to [think of an adult you trust]."

You're being a rubber band, remember? You can bend in new ways without snapping or breaking. Ask for help when you need it.

Flexing (being flexible) is something that you'll need to practice at home and in therapy. It's part of managing the symptoms of ASD. The more you practice, the more flexible you'll be. And that means you'll feel good more often.

Look back at "Signs That You're Feeling Good" on page 162. That's what you're aiming for—feelings of calm and confidence, even when you're bending and stretching. You can do it!

Whenever you're faced with those hard-to-handle feelings, picture your Emotions Toolbox. Use the tools to help you start to feel better:

| Breathe! | Tune in to what you're feeling and why. | Talk to someone— get help. | Flex! |

With time and practice, some of those "bad" feelings may happen less often, and you'll have more good feelings more of the time.

Jackson's Story

Jackson is in the fourth grade and has autism. He spends most of the school day with his regular fourth-grade class. He has an aide, or helper, with him part of the day.

One thing Jackson struggles with is leaving the classroom to go to other places in the school. Jackson hates the hallways—they're *so* loud, and the noise hurts his ears. He hears footsteps, voices, doors opening and closing, bells dinging. For Jackson, the hallways have too much movement and confusion. He gets nervous and upset.

It's Wednesday, which means Jackson has gym. He doesn't like going to gym because he has to walk through a bunch of hallways to the other side of the school. He knows that when he gets there, the gym itself will be loud and full of too much action. Kids will be screaming. Balls will fly through the air. He never knows what might come at him. But whatever it is, it won't be good.

Usually, getting to gym makes him feel so anxious that he slaps himself on the head and tries to run away. But today Jackson and his aide are trying something new to make gym a little easier. They're going to leave for gym class five minutes earlier than the other kids. This means the hall will be clearer, and Jackson will have extra time to try to relax.

As he and his aide walk down the hall, Jackson stays quiet and tries to think about what his doctor taught him about relaxing: take big, deep breaths very slowly and focus his thoughts on a calm place. He does that now. He breathes in and out. "Stay calm," he tells himself.

When he gets to the gym, Jackson sits in the corner, breathing deeply, waiting for the other kids to arrive. His aide smiles at him.

The quiet hallway helped, Jackson thinks to himself. *Maybe the deep breathing will too.*

Chapter 17

"Stims"

> I never sat still; I bobbed and weaved
> and bounced. . . . Most of the time, I stayed alone,
> in my own little world, apart from my peers.

—John Elder Robison, from his memoir, *Look Me in the Eye*

People who write about their autism often tell of a deep need for rhythmic motion and repetition. These repeated motions are what experts refer to as "self-stimulatory behaviors," or "stims." When people use stims, it's called "stimming." Maybe you do some of these:

- rocking back and forth
- flapping your arms or flicking your hands
- banging your head or tapping your fingers on a surface
- twirling or spinning around and around
- humming
- rubbing a piece of cloth or another object
- staring at patterns or observing objects that spin
- lining up objects in a particular order
- dangling string or other objects in front of your eyes, or looking at things from the corners of your eyes
- picking at parts of your body (nose, fingernails, pimples, scabs)
- pacing or walking on your toes
- licking or mouthing objects
- asking the same question over and over, or repeating favorite words
- whatever else you may do repetitively that's unique to you

171

Chastain's Story

Chastain is a third grader who has autism. He likes string a lot, and he carries it everywhere—something he's done his whole life. His mom has pictures of him at two years old holding string in his hands.

When he was younger, Chastain liked to wave the string in front of his eyes. But once he started school, the other kids couldn't understand why Chastain always had his string. Sometimes, they'd tease him when he'd take out his special string and give it a wave. He learned to keep his string in his pocket. Throughout the school day, he'd put his hand in his pocket to make sure the string was there. Touching the string felt good.

This morning when Chastain gets to school, he reaches into his pocket. He can't find his string. He knows he had it earlier. Now he's worried. He looks in his backpack. No string. He looks in his desk. No string. Chastain starts to cry. He *has* to have his special string!

He goes into the hallway to calm down, but he's crying so loud his teacher sends him to the office. The health aide calls Chastain's mom, because he can't stop crying. His mom arrives to take him home. When Chastain gets in the car he's still upset. That's when he sees it—his string! It's right there on the floor of the car, where it must have fallen out that morning.

Chastain picks up his string, gives it a happy wave, and asks his mom if he can go back into the school. He knows he can stay calm. The day will go better now that he has what he needs.

Stims are often done automatically, without your noticing. But sometimes, you might stim on purpose to calm yourself down or deal with worries or boredom. Stims may be your way of feeling "safe" because stimming is familiar and soothing.

Everyone has habits of some sort—some of yours may just happen to be stims. People with ASD stim the way "typical" people twirl their hair, bite their fingernails, or tap their feet. But if everybody has habits, how come stims get a special name? And why are stims often seen as something you need to stop doing or "control"?

Those are tough questions! The answers differ, depending on who you talk to. Parents, doctors, behavior therapists, teachers, and other experts all have points of view. So do people with ASD. Here are some of the different ideas:

- Teachers may notice that a student's stims are a distraction in the classroom. In their view too much stimming might interfere with everyone's learning.

- Many behavior experts say that stims set a child apart. The behaviors look "odd." They may lead to teasing from other children. According to these experts, if the goal is to increase positive social behaviors, then stimming needs to be done less often. (Or at least not in social situations.)

- Sometimes stims become a medical issue. Kids might pick their nose until it bleeds. Or they may scratch their skin until sores develop. Kids who bang their head are at risk of injury.

- In some families, parents and other family members might say that stimming is "annoying," "pointless," or even "harmful." That can seem really unfair! But perhaps it's the family's way of protecting their loved one. They want the child to fit in and feel comfortable.

- In other families, the parents are more accepting of stims. They may see stimming as a symptom, a quirk, or something that simply comes and goes.

- Occupational therapists (OTs) look at how stims connect to the senses. They ask, "What does the stim do for the person's sensory system?" or "What sensory input is the person craving or creating?" (You can read more about the senses in Chapter 3.)

- Lots of people with ASD say that stimming is really soothing and relaxing. Some say that stims help them focus or think better. They wonder, *Why can't autistic behaviors become an accepted part of the world we all share?*

As you can see, there are many different opinions. Even the people on your team of helpers (see Chapter 7) might disagree about this topic. It's easy to get confused about stims or to get confused about who's really the "expert."

Well, maybe you can become your *own* expert here. Think about whether your stimming might be:

- a way to wake up your brain and body
- a way to soothe yourself and relax
- how you get rid of pent-up energy and emotions
- a symptom you'd like to learn to handle
- part of who you are—something you're not ready or willing to change
- a result of your unique sensory needs

Maybe your different stims create different feelings at different times of day. How can you find out? By noticing when you do them. Keep a notebook with you so you can write down the stims you catch yourself doing. Or ask an adult to point them out. This way, you'll learn more about yourself. You'll start to tune in to your emotions and your unique ways of handling them. You'll also get a better understanding of what your stims do for you.

Depending on how you feel about this, a parent, family member, or therapist could make a video of you when you're stimming. Then you can look at the video later and decide what you think. Is the stim something you want to change? Do you want to do it less often? Would you like to do it only in private, so you're not stimming at school or when you're with friends? You can figure out your answers to these questions by thinking them over and talking to adults you trust.

Maybe stims aren't a big concern for you at this time. As you get older, some of your stims might go away on their own. Or, your feelings about them may change.

To work on these behaviors, here are some ideas to try:

Keep them private. Stim in your room or just at home.

Have a secret signal. Ask a family member to give you a secret signal if you stim in public or with friends without being aware of it. (A signal works better than saying, "Stop doing that!") The person could tap you on the shoulder, touch your hand, or whisper in your ear.

Try a different behavior. Find a different way to get the same feeling that stimming gives you. For example, if you like to tap, maybe you'd enjoy drumming. If you hum, try singing along to recorded music or using a karaoke machine or game. If you pace, you could try jogging or walking on a treadmill. If you like doing things with your hands, play with puppets, do crochet, or tap some piano keys. Experiment with different types of art.

Do high-energy activities. Get the sensory input you need by doing activities that offer lots of stimulation: Bounce on a trampoline. Swing at the park. Rock back and forth in a rocking chair. Get a spinning chair you can use at home (sit in it or just watch it go around). Do somersaults, roll in the grass, or wrestle. Figure out what your body and brain *need*—then do it.

Work on relaxation techniques. Learning these will give you different ways to calm yourself. Chapter 19 discusses many ways to relax.

> I like to set up my action figures to match what happens in my video games. I imagine the game in my head over and over. While I'm doing that, I put my face very close to my action figures and move them with my hands so they do what's in my head. It's almost like I watch the action figures while I watch the game in my mind. I like the way this repeats. I call it 'staging.' It's fun for me when I'm alone, and I feel good when I do it.
>
> —10-year-old boy

Chapter 18

Toilet Time

Our bodies are amazing: they can run, leap, think, sleep, talk, smile, and laugh. They're built to be efficient, well-run machines. One thing many machines need in order to work well is a source of fuel. For example, the fuel for cars is gasoline, while the fuel for humans is *food* (see Chapter 22 for more about that). All those fruits, vegetables, and other foods you eat each day turn into energy, which helps you work and play.

As a car uses fuel, it produces waste in the form of exhaust from the tail pipe. Bodies produce waste too. Body waste includes *urine* (liquid waste, which is made by your kidneys) and *feces* (solid waste made in your intestines). Maybe you use other words to describe these waste products, like *pee* and *poop* or *BM* (for bowel movement). In this chapter, we're mostly going to say pee and poop, to keep it simple.

Going to the bathroom is a basic human function, but that doesn't mean it's easy and problem-free. Many kids with ASD have difficulty with *toileting* (as experts refer to it). This chapter talks about some of these toilet troubles and what you can do if you need help. If you don't have problems in this area, you may want to skip to another chapter.

Bathroom Basics

Bathrooms can be scary or uncomfortable places if you have ASD. Some kids don't like the cold surfaces of toilets, sinks, and bathroom floors. Other kids hate the loud, echoing noises—especially the sounds of flushing. Maybe you're worried about germs, or using the toilet paper correctly, or having someone walk in on you. All of these issues lead to feeling anxious, which makes bathroom time more stressful.

Plus, not all bathrooms are exactly like the one you have at home. At home, you know the sound of the flush, how to lock the door, and how the toilet paper comes off the roll. You know how to turn on the faucet afterward to wash your hands. You can find the soap and a towel. But at school, it's a whole different bathroom. The flushing noise is louder. The toilet paper dispenser may be harder to use. And there's a lot less privacy. If you're in the boys' bathroom, there are urinals, which you don't have at home. Because things are different from home, you might not want to use the bathrooms at school unless you really need to go.

Some kids with ASD have a hard time with public bathrooms at restaurants, theaters, and other places. Some places have huge bathrooms with rows and rows of stalls. They can be intimidating! You might discover you can't work the lock on the door . . . or the toilet seat is dirty . . . or you can't even locate the flusher to figure out how it works. Then there are all the smells—you know how bad it can get. And what about those portable toilets at parks and playgrounds? Public bathrooms at crowded places can be a real challenge.

Bathroom problems can be hard to talk about too. We've known kids with ASD who have toileting challenges that go on for a long time. Why? Because the kids kept their problem a secret or didn't realize they could ask an adult for help.

Alisha was very bothered by the loud noises in her school bathroom. The sound of the toilet flushing hurt her ears and echoed everywhere. If she had to poop, she'd get worried because she knew she'd need to be in the bathroom longer. That meant hearing the sounds even more. Instead of going, she'd hold it until she got home, even if she had horrible stomach pain as a result. This made it more difficult to poop later on, because by the time she was ready, it hurt to go.

Samir didn't always realize when he needed to pee. He would get so busy or interested in an activity that he didn't seem to notice when his body was telling him something. That meant he would "leak." At times the leaking went through his pants and the other kids noticed. Sometimes the kids said he smelled like pee. Samir didn't want to be known as the guy who smelled. But he didn't know what to do.

Sophie's problems with coordination made it hard for her to wipe after pooping. Sometimes she used big wads of toilet paper and would accidentally clog the toilet. That scared her. Sometimes she used too little toilet paper and didn't do a good enough job of getting herself clean. She thought it was gross when she got poop on her fingers or underwear by mistake. She didn't want to talk about it, but she needed help.

If you have *any* kind of bathroom problem, don't try to hide it or ignore it. This will only make the problem worse. Something that Alisha, Samir, and Sophie all had in common was that they finally told an adult about their challenges. This meant help was on the way!

Alisha's mom knew about the problems with going to the bathroom at school. Together, they came up with a plan. They talked to the principal and got permission for Alisha to bring her music player to school to use only in the privacy of the bathroom stall. When Alisha had to go to the bathroom, she brought the music player with her and put on the headphones to block out the noise. This helped her relax and made it possible for her to go. What a relief!

Samir and his dad talked about the "leak" problem. They realized it might help if Samir went to the bathroom on a schedule. Then he would be less likely to wait too long to pee. At home, he would use the toilet every hour, even if he didn't feel like he needed to. At school, he followed a routine: He went to the bathroom before his first class started, right before lunch, and after his afternoon gym class. He also brought an extra pair of underwear and pants to keep in his locker in case of an accident. Then he could change his clothes if needed.

Sophie decided to talk to her mom. Her mom understood and made a special point of showing her daughter how much toilet paper was enough, and how much was too much. She told Sophie it was okay to flush after using a couple handfuls of toilet paper, even if she wasn't completely done wiping. After the first flush, she could use more toilet paper as needed, and then flush once again. (They called this a "two-flusher.") Her mom also bought moist wipes to keep by the toilet so Sophie could get herself cleaner. Now Sophie felt more confident.

Bathroom challenges affect a lot of kids with ASD, so you're not alone. If you talk to your mom or dad, your doctor, or your teacher, a plan can be worked out. Some kids have a special bathroom plan at school. For example, the student might only use the bathroom when it's less busy, or an aide might come along to help. Often, there's a different, more private bathroom to use, like in the health office.

If public restrooms are a problem for you, you might look for family restrooms that are set apart from the men's room and women's room. Family bathrooms often have more space so that parents can be in the stall with their kids. These bathrooms might be more private or quiet.

Pee Problems

Many kids—not only those with ASD—have different types of problems when it comes to peeing. Some kids have trouble getting to the bathroom on time. Some forget to go, and then wet their pants. Another common problem is bedwetting, which can happen to kids of any age.

Take a Look!
Some kids with ASD forget that bathroom time is private time. Be sure to shut the door so other people won't see what you're doing in there. Remember to flush too. (No one really wants to see what you've left behind!)

The first step in dealing with either challenge is going to the doctor to find out if there might be a physical problem. Special tests can be done to find out. If everything is in working order, then the problems might be a result of something else.

Forgetting to Go

The best way to fix this problem is to set up a bathroom schedule for yourself, with help from a parent or doctor. (A schedule also helps if you have poop accidents because you've waited too long to get to a bathroom.)

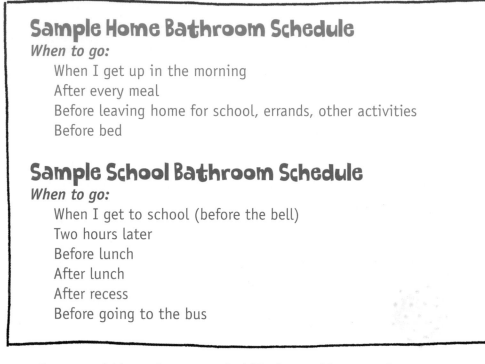

Sample Home Bathroom Schedule
When to go:
When I get up in the morning
After every meal
Before leaving home for school, errands, other activities
Before bed

Sample School Bathroom Schedule
When to go:
When I get to school (before the bell)
Two hours later
Before lunch
After lunch
After recess
Before going to the bus

For some kids and teens with ASD, the problems with peeing are a result of missing the signals their bodies are sending. Your body "tells" you when you have to pee. You'll notice your bladder feels full, for example, or you'll have a sensation of pressure in that area. Anytime your bladder feels full, listen to that message. STOP what you're doing, even if it's fun or you think you're too busy and can wait. Peeing *as soon as* you feel that urge teaches you to listen closely to your body.

Bedwetting

If you're wetting the bed at night, that's a challenge too. Bedwetting is more common than you may think. And it can be frustrating. You need to know that you don't wet the bed because you're "lazy," "dumb," or "a baby." Wetting the bed often happens because the connections between someone's brain and body aren't fully working yet. The connections usually work better during the day, when the person is awake. But if the person is sleeping, the signals from the brain to the body "sleep" too! Maybe the person is a heavy sleeper, and sleeps too soundly or deeply to wake up to go to the bathroom. Or maybe the "I need to pee" signal happens, but not quickly enough for the person to wake and get to the toilet in time.

If you sometimes wet the bed or wet it every night, there's help for you. Here's what helps many kids and teens who wet the bed:

Fluid restriction. This means you cut way back on the amount of liquids you drink from late afternoon into the evening. Drinking less at this time of day means you'll produce less urine at night. Your bladder

won't be as full when you go to bed, so you'll be less likely to wet the bed (or less pee will come out if you do). Try not to drink anything at all two hours before bedtime. It's especially good to avoid caffeine (drinks like soda, coffee, or tea), because it makes you have to go more.

Schedules. Set up an evening bathroom schedule so you "go" frequently before bedtime. For example, you might make a point of peeing every hour from the late afternoon until bedtime. If your parents stay up later than you do, you could have them wake you right before they go to sleep. That way, you can get up and pee one last time before you fall into a deep sleep.

Bedwetting alarms. These devices wake you up when you start to pee in your bed. (They're designed to make a noise or a vibration the moment they sense liquid.) The alarm wakes you, which allows you to stop peeing and get to a toilet before wetting the bed completely. After frequent use, the alarm trains your brain to pay closer attention to the signal from your bladder. Alarms usually attach to your pajamas and have a wire that goes to your underpants—if any part of the wire gets wet, the alarm alerts you.

Alarms are safe and can be helpful for some people. Ask your doctor for a recommendation. One thing to know ahead of time is that bedwetting alarms can be *very* loud. Some kids with ASD get so scared or upset from the noise that it's hard to go back to sleep afterward. However, many alarms have a vibration setting that can be used instead.

Medications. There are medications that can help stop bedwetting. They require a prescription from a doctor. Some of these medications are taken every night. Others are taken only on nights when they're needed (like if the person has a sleepover or is going camping).

Pee pads. Your dad or mom can buy special pads that absorb urine. One kind goes inside your underwear. Another is made of waterproof material and goes on the bed over the sheets. You can also consider adult diapers or the extra-large size of kids' "pull-ups."

Bedwetting can be embarrassing and frustrating. Here's the good news: **Help is available.** Your doctor can give you advice, or you and a parent can find books or websites about bedwetting. There's more good news: The problem will lessen as you get older and the connections in your brain get stronger.

Note for Adults

Bedwetting isn't a sign that your child "isn't trying." Kids who wet the bed need help, not anger or disappointment. Even when you're exhausted, try not to yell or make your child feel guilty if you're changing sheets in the middle of the night or every morning. This only makes the situation more frustrating for everyone in the family. Instead, buy several absorbent protective pads for the bed. Use easy-to-wash blankets instead of down comforters or bedding that must be dry-cleaned. It's simpler that way.

Poop Problems

Having bowel movements is just one of those things we all have to do—it's part of life. But for some people, it's a part that's hard to deal with.

Many kids with ASD have difficulty with pooping because it's a sensory activity. There are noises and smells involved, plus internal feelings that are hard for some kids to handle. This can lead to resistance: In other words, you try to avoid pooping or put it off until you absolutely can't wait any longer. This isn't good for your body, though. Your body *has* to get rid of waste to stay healthy.

Here are some ideas that may work for you. But first, talk to a parent about the trouble you're having in the bathroom.

- **Try to keep a schedule.** Poop first thing in the morning or right after breakfast, if you can. (That way you're still at home and can more easily relax.) Eating a meal often signals to your body that it's time to get rid of the waste.

- **Keep yourself hydrated.** This makes it easier to poop. Drink lots of water during the day.

- **Exercise regularly.** Movement helps the poop make its way through your system. The more you move, the more your poop moves!

- **Take your time.** A bowel movement is more likely to occur if you're relaxed. Take a book or a portable music or video player with you into the bathroom and sit for a while.

- **Fix the sensory problems.** If the toilet seat feels too hard or cold, ask your parents to get one made of softer material that stays warmer. Put a portable heater in the bathroom if you get cold sitting with your pants down. If you don't like the smells, then you can use sprays or deodorizers while you "go."

- **Change your diet.** Sometimes, kids with ASD get *constipated* (meaning, it's hard to poop) because their diets are so limited. Maybe they're mostly eating hot dogs, French fries, cheese, and milk—which tend to be constipating. Chapter 22 talks about the importance of eating healthy foods. If you're constipated, your poop might get so big that it's painful to get it out, or you might start having stomach cramps. To avoid this, eat fresh fruits and veggies and drink more water.

If you try these suggestions and still have problems, it's important to talk to a doctor. The doctor will check to make sure everything is working properly. If needed, there are medications you can take to help keep your poop soft and make it easier to have a BM.

The Final Flush

In general, kids with ASD just need more practice when it comes to going to the bathroom. It may sound strange, but toileting is a *skill*—just like other self-care skills such as bathing or brushing your teeth. Give yourself time. Ask your family to be patient with you. Don't be afraid to get help.

Chapter 19

Learning to Relax

"Relax!" "Chill out!" "Take it easy!" Do people ever say that to you? (Like when you seem nervous, upset, or frustrated?) Sure, it would be great if you could instantly relax the moment someone suggests you do so—but *that* probably doesn't happen. Often, hearing you need to relax can make you feel even more stressed out.

Having ASD may mean you're more anxious than the average person. Why? Maybe it's sensory issues (see Chapter 3). Maybe it's because you have trouble in social situations, and that makes you feel nervous. Or, maybe you have more stress hormones floating around in your brain and body. Whatever the reason, the stress is there, and it doesn't go away just because someone *tells* you to relax.

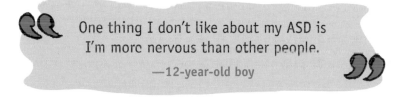

One thing I don't like about my ASD is
I'm more nervous than other people.

—12-year-old boy

This chapter is about *how* to relax. Did you know that relaxation is a skill you can learn? Once you know how to do it, you can use this skill to stay calmer in situations that cause you stress. Here you'll read three ideas to help you develop this skill. Some of the ideas work best at home, and some can be used at school or anywhere.

A Calm-Down Space

At times when you're stressed, scared, angry, or frustrated, it helps to have a place where you can calm down. Think about a place at home where you can go to feel peaceful. Ask a parent to help you design a special place—a Calm-Down Space—just for you. It doesn't have to be fancy to work well.

Your Calm-Down Space can be:
- your bed
- a beanbag or cozy chair
- a cleared space inside a closet
- a blanket-covered table you can fit under
- another comfy spot at home

> I 'crash' on my beanbag in my room.
> I flop onto it a bunch of times. *Crash-crash*.
> It helps me feel calmer.
>
> —11-year-old girl

It's really important to get some help finding this place and making it yours. That way, when you go to your Calm-Down Space, your family will know where you are. You'll be safe there.

How to make your Calm-Down Space comfortable:
- Have a few blankets and pillows handy.
- Keep a music player and headphones there so you can listen to relaxing music, like instrumental jazz or classical.
- Use noise-blocking headphones or ear plugs.
- Turn the lights low or off. (If you can't change the lighting, use sunglasses if you'd like.)
- Have something to hold close, like a stuffed animal, a small pillow, or a body pillow.
- Keep a water bottle handy.
- Have a journal and pencil for writing or drawing.

A Calm-Down Space can be so relaxing you may want to spend all day there. But it's important to allow time for family and friends too!

What you can do when you need to calm down:

- cry
- yell into a pillow
- flop into the beanbag
- snuggle under the blankets
- write about or draw your feelings

- take a nap
- think, dream, remember, wish, or pray
- try Belly Breathing (described below)

Belly Breathing

It's hard to believe, but something as simple as *breathing* can help you feel less stressed and more in charge of your emotions. Belly Breathing is a special way of controlling how you breathe, so you feel calmer and more relaxed.

You can use this type of breathing when you're upset, worried, or stressed. It's a tool to help you calm down and get a handle on your emotions before they spin out of control.

Belly Breathing does three great things:

1. It calms your nerves.

2. It relaxes your muscles.

3. It helps release *endorphins,* or chemicals that reduce pain, increase energy, and help you feel positive and happy.

Take a Look!

Sometimes, kids with ASD leave their home seeking a quiet place to help them settle down when they're upset. That's really scary for the family, because they know their loved one could get lost or hurt. Other times, kids might hide somewhere inside the home, yard, or car to get a little peace and quiet—and then not realize that the family is looking everywhere for them. **Make sure your Calm-Down Space is a place everyone at home knows about.** Use it when you need to. Let your family know that you like to be alone there, and when you're ready to come out and talk, you will.

Here's how to Belly Breathe:

- Use your imagination to pretend you have a balloon in your belly.
- Put one hand on top of your belly.
- Breathe in *slowly* through your nose. As you do this, count to three, pausing in between each number (1, *pause*, 2, *pause*, 3). Feel the imaginary balloon filling with air.
- Breathe out *slowly* through your mouth. Count to five, pausing between each number. Imagine that the balloon is getting flat. Imagine your bad feelings leaving your body as you breathe out.
- Repeat the Belly Breathing several times. Notice your muscles relaxing as you do. *Ahhhhh . . .*

Belly Breathing is even more relaxing and fun if you have a little something extra to help you—especially when you're learning to do it. For example, you can use a colorful pinwheel that turns as you breathe on it. (You can find pinwheels at a dollar store or drugstore.) Or, you can get a small container of bubble stuff and blow through the wand as you breathe out. Watch the bubbles peacefully drift through the air.

A Relaxation Exercise

Sometimes, you might want to do a longer relaxation exercise that helps clear your mind and calm your body. Use the following one any time you want to relax from head to toe.

Ask a parent or another trusted adult to read each of the steps as you do them. After you've done the sequence many times, you'll probably have it memorized and can do it on your own.

1. Find a quiet place (if possible, do this outside because the fresh air feels great).
2. Lie down on the grass (or floor, if you're indoors) and get comfortable.
3. Close your eyes, but don't fall asleep.

4. Breathe deeply, focusing on your breath going in and out. Count to five as you breathe in, and count backward from five as you breathe out. Take your time. Pause between each number so the counting doesn't go too fast.

5. When you feel calmer, continue breathing deeply. This time say the word *relax* as you breathe in and out.

6. In time with your breathing, begin to relax your muscles from head to toe. Start with your forehead. Tense those muscles as you inhale. Then relax them as you exhale.

7. Continue tensing and relaxing your muscles, moving downward from your head to your neck and shoulders, to your arms, stomach, legs, and feet.

8. When you've reached your toes, tense and relax them. Then take a rest. Keep breathing deeply.

9. Slowly open your eyes. You are now relaxed.

10. Enjoy this feeling!

Don't wait until you're stressed to learn the techniques in this chapter. Practice them at home when you have time and when an adult can help guide you. Then, once you know how to do Belly Breathing and deep breathing, you can use these tools whenever you're angry, scared, nervous, or upset. If you have an OT (occupational therapist), that person can show you other ways to calm down and relax. You may also want to learn yoga, a form of exercise that involves stretching and paying special attention to the breath.

Chapter 20

Is There Medicine for ASD?

Doctors and other experts believe that autism is a medical condition. Many medical conditions have cures or treatments. But how about ASD?

Today there is no proven cure for autism. But there *are* treatments that can make a positive difference in your life.

Maybe you're already doing therapy treatments to help improve how you communicate and get along with others. Your therapies might take place at home, school, or a special therapy center that helps people who have disabilities. Many families work hard to find treatments to help relieve the symptoms of ASD and make life better. You're probably working hard yourself, trying to gain new skills.

In the search for ways to help, your family might see a doctor who suggests a medication that focuses on (targets) certain symptoms. Only a medical professional, usually a doctor, can prescribe (order the use of) medication. Most likely, the doctor will ask a lot of questions about you: Do you sleep well at night? Is it easy or difficult for you to pay attention in school? Do you have a lot of stress or worries? How do you handle them? Do you have trouble managing anger? The doctor's job is to get information about your physical and mental health. This helps the doctor better understand you and how medication ("meds" for short) might help.

If you need a medication, or if your family agrees that it's time to try one, you might be confused and worried at first. You might wonder what the medication looks like and how it will make you feel. Your doctor can answer these questions, so be sure to ask (or have a parent or caregiver ask with you).

Usually, meds come in a pill or capsule you swallow or crush, or a liquid you drink. But some even come in the form of a bandage you wear. Some people take a medication once a day, while others take it several times a day. In some cases, more than one type of medication may be prescribed.

Getting Medication: Three Important Steps

Step 1: Deciding which symptom to target

Remember back in Chapter 1, where you learned the symptoms of autism? You read that differences in your brain make it more difficult for you to communicate, be social, and have a wide variety of interests. ASD also affects your senses: sight, smell, hearing, touch, taste, and more. Does this mean you can take a medication to make you "talk better" or find more friends? Nope, it doesn't work that way. The symptoms that medications target are much more specific.

This is why a doctor has to ask a lot of questions before helping your family decide if medication may be an option for you. Most medications prescribed for ASD will focus on treating particular kinds of ASD symptoms. Here are four common categories of symptoms:

1. **Attention and focus.** Some kids on the spectrum have trouble sitting still, getting organized, or paying attention. They might do things too quickly without thinking first.

2. **Worries and repetitive thoughts.** This category includes having trouble being alone, or feeling nervous or anxious when making changes or being in new places. Kids with these kinds of symptoms might do the same thing over and over or ask things again and again.

3. **Being too aggressive.** Lots of arguing, yelling, and hitting are *aggressive* behaviors. Kids with problems in this area might also cry uncontrollably or hit or scratch themselves when they're scared or upset.

4. **Sleep issues.** Some young people with autism spectrum disorder have trouble getting to sleep at night. Or they may wake up in the night or too early in the morning.

Each type of symptom calls for a different kind of medicine. You, your parents, your teachers, and all your other helpers play a role in thinking about symptoms to target. You can start by making a list of things you struggle with on a daily basis. A parent can note what gives you trouble at home. Your teachers can offer suggestions for what might help you do better in school. With all this information, your doctor can see if the symptoms you most need help with match the list above.

Take a Look!

This chapter talks about medication and the role it may play in ASD. The chapter isn't suggesting you *should* or *should not* use medication. That decision is up to your family, with input from your doctor and other helpers.

Step 2: Discussing meds and possible side effects

The second step is to talk with your doctor about which medications might help your symptoms. You'll also learn what, if any, *side effects* you might experience. Side effects are the unexpected or unintended results of taking a medication. For example, you may take a medication to help you sleep, but then discover it also gives you headaches. Some side effects are mild, but others aren't. Some are temporary, while others last as long as you take the medication. You and your family can talk with the doctor about any questions or concerns you have.

Your doctor will choose from different medications that may target the same symptom and will look at the possible side effects of each one, the dose to take, and the cost. With some medications, it's first necessary to have medical tests to examine your blood or your heart. You may need to go back for further testing while on the medication.

For some people with ASD, other health conditions might be important too. If you're already on medication for any reason, your family needs to report this to any other doctor you see. Then the doctor can make sure *not* to prescribe medications that might not work well with one you're already on.

Step 3: Tracking whether the symptoms improve for you

Follow-up is an important part of taking a new medication. Your doctor—and you and your family—will want to be sure the medication is making a positive difference in your life. It helps if your parent or caregiver keeps a daily log of any changes you experience. Bring the log each time you see the doctor. Show the doctor records of:

- when you started the meds
- what time of day you take them
- any times you've missed taking them
- what improvements you've noticed
- any side effects you may have
- if the side effects are mild or severe, and how long they last

If you have side effects, your doctor may try these different ways of getting rid of them:

- changing the medication
- adjusting the dose
- changing the time of day you take the medication
- asking you to take the medication with food

Your doctor will require you to come back for another appointment. There, you and your family can discuss whether it's a good idea to stay on the medication, try another, or stop medication altogether.

Keep Communicating

Finding a medication can be a long process—a long process that not every family chooses to go through. Your family gets to decide what's best for you.

If you do take medications, *communication* is a very important part of the process. Let your family know how your meds make you feel physically. Are there any side effects, for example? Then your family can tell your doctor what's working and what isn't.

Most of all, be sure to follow the medication instructions your doctor gives you. Go to your appointments too. Together, you, your family, and your doctor can track your progress and figure out what's most helpful to you.

Vicki's Story

Vicki is 8 and has autism. She has *lots* of friends, energy, and interests. Sometimes she feels like her head is going to explode with ideas.

When she's supposed to be doing math, Vicki might be thinking of her favorite hobby: trading wristbands. She has over 200 wristbands. She likes to organize them every night and put some in her backpack for school the next day. She sometimes gets in trouble at school because she can't get her mind off her wristbands.

Vicki's teacher says Vicki talks too much in class, interrupts, and has trouble staying on task. Vicki, her dad, and her teacher meet with the school psychologist to talk about this. Together, they decide it would be a good idea to ask a doctor about medication.

After a few meetings, the doctor prescribes a medication for Vicki that helps with focus and attention. Vicki learns that she might have side effects, like trouble sleeping or changes in her appetite. The doctor also explains that Vicki should tell her dad if she notices any "funny feelings," like not being hungry or getting nervous and upset.

Vicki starts the medication. On the very first day she notices a difference. She can pay attention more easily. She doesn't talk as much. She can wait her turn, and she patiently raises her hand in class instead of interrupting. Her teacher calls Vicki's dad to share the good news.

Vicki likes feeling happy and focused in school. But the hours after school are terrible for her! The medication gradually leaves her system during the day, and then Vicki feels crabby. At home at night, she yells at her sister, cries, and doesn't even want to play with her wristbands.

Her dad calls the doctor about these side effects. Over the next few weeks, Vicki's doctor keeps changing the medication. The dose goes up. It goes down. Sometimes Vicki has to take one pill; other times, two. She starts to feel like a yo-yo—up and down, up and down.

After weeks of adjusting the dose, Vicki's family decides meds aren't the answer. It's more important that Vicki feels good *all* day long, even if it means she has difficulty paying attention in school.

Now Vicki feels like herself again. She knows she has to work harder to focus, but she's trying. And she's decided, with her dad's support, that when she's older she might want to try medication again.

Jamal's Story

Jamal collects, organizes, sorts, counts—and sometimes he can't stop. He likes things to be the same . . . every day.

Today, his mom says they need to go buy him a new pair of shoes. Jamal hates the idea. He runs and hides in his closet. He thinks, *I don't need new shoes! New shoes are always too tight or too loose!*

Outside the closet door, Jamal's mom tries to reassure him. She promises to get him a Lego set if he cooperates. But Jamal can't stand trying on new shoes. He stays in the closet. His mom gives up.

It's not just shoes that are a problem. Jamal's mom has a hard time getting him to do lots of things, even coming to the table at dinner-time. He doesn't like to stop what he's already doing, especially if it's something fun like building with his construction kit.

Jamal and his mom know he has autism. But Jamal's mom feels it's important for him to try new things and not get "stuck" so often. She tells him they're going to the doctor to get some help.

Jamal's doctor knows him well. He understands that Jamal prefers "sameness" and has a hard time moving from one activity to the next. Jamal practices being flexible, but it's getting harder for him to do. The doctor suggests a medication that might help Jamal be less rigid in his thinking and learn to accept change.

Jamal takes this new medication every day, just like his doctor said to do. He and his mom watch for side effects, like trouble sleeping or feeling restless. So far, so good.

One night a few weeks later, Jamal is organizing his Lego collection, thinking about all the awesome things he can build. "Jamal, dinner!" his mom calls.

Jamal runs downstairs, hungry. Then he notices the strange look on his mom's face. For a moment, he's confused. Then his mom smiles. "Jamal, you came right to the table without any fuss!" Jamal smiles back at her, proud of himself.

After dinner, Mom says, "Maybe tomorrow we can buy new shoes?" "I'll think about it," Jamal answers. And he wonders to himself, *Maybe the medication is helping?*

Chapter 21

Move Your Body

So far, you've learned a lot about autism spectrum disorder and how it can affect your brain and body. You're probably starting to better understand your own ASD and how you can manage it, with support from your team of helpers. You've also discovered that you have a few things to handle on a daily basis: your symptoms and sensory issues, for example. Guess what can help you better manage both?

Exercise!

You'll get fitter and feel better—and that's just for starters. Studies show that kids who exercise have stronger muscles, bones, hearts, lungs, and vital organs. Plus, they get better sleep and better grades.

Besides keeping your body in good shape, exercise can help you burn off extra energy or cope with stress. If you start now, healthy exercise habits (and their benefits) can last a lifetime.

Get Active!

The National Association for Sport and Physical Education (NASPE) says that school-age children should get 60 minutes or more of physical activity per day. If you want, you can break up the minutes. For example, you could do four sessions of activity for 15 minutes, or do two sessions lasting 30 minutes. Activities include anything that gets your heart beating faster, or that stretches and strengthens your muscles.

play outside

go for a run, jog, or hike

go to the park or playground

shoot hoops or toss a ball against a wall

take a long walk with your family

learn to do yoga or simple stretches

swim at a community center

play tag or other neighborhood games

run races with your friends

bounce on a trampoline

ride a bike or scooter

make up crazy dances

Use a Wii or Xbox to exercise your whole body—not just your fingers!

What about trying out for a sport or joining a team? Many young people with ASD tend not to be great at team sports. Maybe you happen to be a proud athlete and member of a sports team—if you are, way to go! But if you aren't, that's okay. Team sports may not be your thing. Team sports can be difficult because there's a social aspect to team play. You need to read your teammates' body language. You have to be able to predict what they might do next on the field or court, or what they need *you* to do. Team sports are often loud too. They also call for coordination. Many people with ASD have difficulty moving their bodies in a coordinated way.

Imagine all the steps a baseball pitcher takes to wind up for a pitch: He puts his arms over his head, starts his pitching motion, and turns his body while one arm goes back and around. His opposite foot then strides toward the plate, and he throws the ball forward. Then he quickly gets back into position, ready to field the ball if it's hit. Pitchers do all these steps so smoothly that fans who are watching hardly notice all that's really involved.

If you were doing the pitching, you might have to stop and think about each movement: What your legs must do. Where your right arm should be. Where your left arm needs to go. Where to focus your eyes. How to hold the ball, how to let go, and where to aim. And so on. If your brain has trouble planning the order of the movements, then your body doesn't act on them as quickly or smoothly.

If coordination is a problem for you, you might think of yourself as "clumsy." But it's really an issue of needing extra help, time, and practice. You have to train your brain and body more than the average person—but it *can* be done. Ask a parent, older sibling, or buddy to help you practice swinging a baseball bat, tossing a football, or working on lay-ups at the basketball court. These are great ways to build your strength and get the physical exercise you need.

If you want to play team sports, you can practice the coordination skills your sport needs. It might also be helpful to work on "reading" other people's body language and making eye contact. You can learn more about these communication skills on pages 80–89.

Many kids with ASD prefer solo sports like swimming, tennis, archery, rock climbing, golf, karate, track and field, dance, gymnastics, or tai chi. These sports involve seeing and interacting with other kids too. But your performance is "just yours" and you can work at your own pace. Baseball and softball are often good "compromise" activities. This is because even though they're considered team sports, the focus is mainly on the individual performance of each player.

> To me, [basketball is] the perfect sport for someone who's autistic, because there are all these drills you can do by yourself. You can shoot hoops in your backyard all day long. You can practice your dribble. Whatever you want to work on, you can just work on it and work on it.
>
> —Jason McElwain, from his book *The Game of My Life: A True Story of Challenge, Triumph, and Growing Up Autistic*

To get involved in athletics, see what your school has to offer. Ask your dad or mom to help you find community sports opportunities. Maybe there's a sports program just for kids with special needs. You can also look for a local center for people with disabilities, where you can use a special pool, track, or other equipment. Some communities offer horseback riding therapy for children with ASD or other disabilities.

Looking for more options? Join the YMCA or YWCA. Go to your community's recreation center several times a week. Take lessons (tap dance, martial arts, whatever!). Run around during recess. Participate in gym class at school. Spend lots of time outdoors. Ask neighbors or classmates to

join you on bike rides. Or invite them to go on a walk with you and your dog or play a game of catch. When you're busy doing a physical activity together, conversation is usually less important. This makes things easier if talking and listening are difficult for you.

If motor skills and physical coordination are an issue for you, you may find it helpful to try physical therapy (PT) or occupational therapy (OT). Read more about them on page 49. Both types of therapy are great for improving balance and strengthening the core muscles of your body.

Want to make exercise a part of your daily routine? Try these ideas:

- Make it a rule for yourself. This is especially helpful if you find that life is easier when there are guidelines to follow.
- Put it on your daily schedule, your calendar, or your to-do list each day.
- Give yourself a fun reward afterward, like extra time on your favorite hobby.
- Think of physical activity as something that helps you feel good.

Bonus: Exercise can be a social activity. You'll meet new people if you join a team or take lessons. You can find other kids to hang out with at the community center. If you go to a playground, you're sure to find other kids there too. It's fun to exercise with others. Try it!

Take a Look!

No matter where you are on the autism spectrum, it's important for you to get some exercise. Don't make excuses like "I hate sports" or "I'm no good." Physical activity releases feel-good chemicals called *endorphins* in your brain and body. Exercise also lessens stress, which is especially important for kids with ASD.

Gretchen's Story

Gretchen is 10 and has ASD. Her older brother Ian is a good downhill skier. Gretchen doesn't ski, but she thinks it looks so fun. Her family lives in a state where it snows a lot, and winter sports are a big deal. She's tried skiing before, but it was complicated. First, she had to put on a helmet. It felt heavy and kind of tight. Then there were ski goggles to wear— also tight. Gretchen found it hard to keep the skis pointing straight and to hang onto the poles. The squeaky sound of the snow under the skis made her nervous too. But the scariest thing was the chair lift. Gretchen just couldn't get on it. The chair was so high, and it kept moving. She watched as the chairs swung around and picked people up, carrying them to the top of the hill. They dangled so high in the air! It looked way too dangerous.

So Gretchen decided not to ski, at least for a while. Instead, when her dad and brother ski, she likes to look out the window of the building where people warm up. One day as she does this, she takes a closer look at the chair lift. It's made of tall poles, heavy chains, and turning wheels. Gretchen likes to count, so she starts counting the wheels and the poles. Soon her dad comes to check on her. Gretchen says, "The pulleys and poles work together to get the skiers up the hill." Her dad smiles, and then he says, "If you ride on the lift with me, we can see if you're right." But Gretchen isn't ready for that.

At home later that night, her mom notices that Gretchen seems to have something on her mind. "What's up, Gretchen?"

"I want to ride the chair lift, but I'm scared," Gretchen tells her. "I want to ski, but it's too hard."

Ian and Dad join the conversation. Everyone's excited that Gretchen wants to ski, because they know it's something the whole family could do together. Their dream is to take a trip to the mountains and stay at a ski lodge. There they would spend long days skiing and having fun as a family. Gretchen likes that idea a lot.

Together, the whole family makes a plan: Gretchen can get used to skiing very slowly. She'll start by wearing her brother's helmet and goggles around the house. Then she can take her time getting used to skis. Finally, she can practice riding the ski lift with her dad.

And that's exactly what happens. For a little while each day, Gretchen sits indoors with the helmet and goggles on. She knows she looks funny, but it's all for the ski trip! After a few weeks, she learns to get the skis off and on and walk around with them in the snowy backyard. This takes some coordination, but Gretchen doesn't give up.

Now, she's feeling ready, but she's still scared. She and her dad are at the ski hill. Gretchen has on a helmet, goggles, skis, and a ski jacket like Ian's. The chair lift looms before them. Gretchen's dad talks to the man running the lift. He agrees to slow it down so Gretchen can get on more easily. She holds her dad's hand tight. Here comes the chair . . .

In a flash, she and her dad are on the chair lift. Gretchen closes her eyes and hangs on tight. She's doing it! She's riding through the air like all the other skiers. It's not long before her dad says, "Gretchen, we're at the top—let's get off."

It all happens really fast. Her skis hit the ground, she slides down a little hill, and then she falls on her butt, laughing. She's *at the top*—she can practically see the whole world! Gretchen is so proud of herself. She can't wait to tell Mom and Ian about her ride up the hill.

Now all she has to do is go *down* the hill. She thinks she's ready!

Check Your "Engine"

Imagine for a moment that your body is a car. The engine is what keeps it running. It's time to check that engine of yours. Does it often run too fast or too slow? For example, are there times when you're expected to be calm and quiet (like in the library), but you're zooming around like it's NASCAR? Or, are there times when everyone around you seems to be talking loudly and having tons of fun, and all you want to do is park yourself in a quiet corner?

Sometimes, it probably feels as if your engine speed doesn't match the "driving conditions" around you. At times, your engine may be out of control, out of rhythm, or out of gas. Want to know what can help?

There are things you can do to rev up your engine or bring it down to a nice purr. The chart on page 205 explains more about "checking your engine" and giving it what it needs. This chart includes ideas that many OTs and PTs use during their sessions with kids. You and your parents can pull out the chart whenever you need an engine check. You can make a photocopy or download a copy at freespirit.com/SGforASD.

How to "Speed Up" or "Slow Down"

The day goes more smoothly when your engine speed fits what the situation demands of you. For example, you might be at a "60" just before gym class at school—perfect timing! When you head back to class afterward, you might be at a "40" and ready to learn. Late in the day, sitting on the school bus, you might be at a "20," which helps you stay calm on the ride home—*ahhhh*.

What if you're still at "20" when you get home from school, and your mom expects you to start your homework? Roadside emergency service needed! Better get the chart and show your mom how you feel.

Or, what if you're at "80" when you get to school the next morning? This makes it hard to settle down and focus. You need ideas for putting on the brakes.

There are lots of ways to slow down your engine or rev it up, depending on what speed you need. Here are some tips to help you get in the right gear.

Move around (a lot). Maybe you need to bounce, run, jog, spin, tumble, or climb. Jump on a trampoline or an old couch (ask permission first), play tug-of-war with a friend, or go to a park. If you have to stay indoors, climb up and down stairs. Even chores can help you get physical: rake leaves or sweep the floor.

Move around (a little). If you're in class and have the urge to move, stand up if you can. Take a bathroom break so you can walk down the hall, or maybe get a drink of water. Just ask your teacher first. Maybe your IEP (see page 138) allows you to take breaks during school in a quiet place. Use those breaks to move your body so you feel better.

Some classrooms have ball chairs you can sit and gently bounce on. Others have sensory areas you can use during breaks (if you have permission). If moving around isn't possible, you could go out in the hall to briefly stretch your neck, shoulders, arms, and legs.

Check Your Engine

Your Engine Speed	How do you feel at this speed?
80: Too fast, out of control (you might crash!) 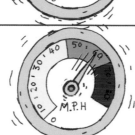	You might feel disorganized, angry, or scared. You may want to run or fight, or to tune out and shut down. Your behavior might get too wild. Or you might feel like you can't deal with anyone or anything for a while. This is a good time for a break.
60: High energy 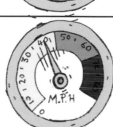	You might feel excited, energetic, and ready for a challenge. This is a good time to do some physical activity.
40: Running smooth, humming and purring 	You might feel confident, happy, and tuned in. This is a good time for some mental activity, like learning.
20: Running slow but still chugging along 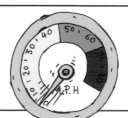	You may not feel you're at your best, but you're getting somewhere—slowly. This is a good time for quiet activities, where people won't expect a lot out of you. If you still have homework or chores to do, you could try a little exercise so your engine speeds up again. (Aim for "40"—"80" is too fast.)
0: Running too slow— you need a little push	You might feel bored or sad. It may be hard to do what a teacher, parent, or therapist tells you to. This is a good time to ask for some help and support.

Do "resistance work." You can work your muscles through *resistance.* How? Push your arms against a wall. Or pull something (like a rolling backpack). Carry some heavy books. Jump up and down, or roll around in the grass or on the floor.

When you don't have much room to move around, try palm presses: Interlock your fingers and press your palms together, with your elbows up and out at shoulder level.

Resistance activities like these help your body feel more organized and get your engine numbers up or down.

Find your rhythm. Many people with autism find that rhythmic body movements calm them and help block out noise and activity. Maybe you rock back and forth or flap your hands and arms for this purpose. Sometimes, you might pace when you're anxious or bored. If pacing, rocking, or flapping are things your school or family are comfortable with, they can help you steady your engine.

Some teachers and families will want you to find other ways to get that soothing feeling. Here are some examples of different things that may relax and calm you: swinging, bouncing on a workout ball, rocking in a rocking chair, dancing, or swinging back and forth on a hammock. Some families get mini trampolines for year-round use. Others get an indoor swing that can be safely hung from the ceiling.

Keep your hands busy. If you feel bored or fidgety, it helps to do something with your hands. For example, doodle, draw, or play with clay or a stress ball. If you need something that won't draw much attention, carry a straw, twist tie, or paper clip in your pocket. You can bend and twist it in your pocket or pull it out and bend it in your hands.

Keep your mouth busy. Sometimes, you might feel like you need to eat a crunchy food, suck on ice cubes or hard candies, or chew something chewy. Doing something with your mouth can help your brain focus. At home, chew sugarless bubblegum. At school, see if you can chew gum during times when you need to wake up or keep your mouth busy. Keep a water bottle at your desk so you always have something to drink. You can talk more about this with your OT at school or at a therapy center. OTs usually have lots of great ideas for helping kids with sensory issues that have to do with the mouth.

Check your ears. Sometimes, you might feel too revved up by the amount of noise around you. Loud noises might startle you. And they might leave you feeling jumpy long after the sound has passed. At other times, even everyday background noises (like the TV, other people's voices, or a ticking clock) might bother you a lot.

It's helpful to keep a pair of ear muffs or ear plugs handy. If you're in the car or on the bus, use headphones to listen to soothing music. Or, choose rhythmic sounds such as ocean waves or falling rain.

Go someplace quiet. Chapter 19 talks about creating a Calm-Down Space at home—a place where you can go for some peace and quiet when you feel wound up. Keep soothing items there, like blankets and pillows, so you have what you need to feel cozy.

Relax. Even though school and therapy help you succeed in life, they can be tiring, and sometimes it's just hard to keep going. At times like these, a break is essential. After a long, *active* day, you can:

Take a warm bath or hot shower.

Get a hug from someone you love.

Take a nap.

Hold someone's hand.

Curl up with a good book.

Turn off the overhead lights, or put on an eye mask for a while.

Ask a family member to rub your feet or lightly tickle your back.

Snuggle up with your cat, or pet your dog.

Watch your fish swim around and around in their tank.

Chapter 22

Feed Your Body

If you read Chapter 21, you've already learned how to take care of your "engine." Now it's time to check your fuel supply. Your engine's fuel isn't gasoline—it's *food.* The human body needs food to survive. Normal body functions like digestion and breathing rely on energy from food. Food contains essential *nutrients* that get absorbed by your bloodstream. There they are changed into blood sugar and delivered to your cells.

What are nutrients? They're the parts of food that provide your body with the fuel it needs to run. They include vitamins, minerals, proteins, complex carbohydrates, and *good* fats and oils. (Bad fats and oils are the ones found in snack foods and sweets.)

A good diet keeps you healthy and strong—but it also helps you better manage the symptoms of your ASD. Why? Because ASD affects your brain. Think of your brain as a hungry part of your body. It craves nutrients! It needs them to function in the best way it can.

Getting Enough Nutrients

Different nutrients do different jobs in your brain:

Vitamins. They're found in fruits, veggies, juices and milk, tofu, and enriched breakfast cereals, and in the form of supplements.

what they do:
- Keep your brain cells alive and healthy.
- Keep your brain cells "awake" so you're alert and thinking clearly.
- Boost your mood.

Minerals. They're found in fruits, veggies, juices and milk, nuts, meat, fish, and enriched grains, and in the form of supplements.

what they do:

- Help your brain send messages back and forth.
- Act as "bursts of energy" that help different parts of your brain communicate.

Proteins. They're found in eggs, meat, fish, nuts and seeds, veggies, tofu, soy, whole-grain foods, nut butters, milk, and other dairy products such as yogurt and cheese.

what they do:

- Build muscles.
- Become protein "messengers" inside your brain and body.

Good **fats and oils.** They're found in raw fruits and veggies, eggs, nuts and seeds, fish (especially salmon), olive oil, and grapeseed oil. Some good fats—like fish oil—are available as supplements.

what they do:

- Keep the walls of your brain cells healthy and flexible.
- Keep your nerves healthy.
- Boost your mood.

Take a Look!
Bad fats and oils—the ones found in French fries, potato chips, corn chips, deep-fried foods, donuts, brownies, cookies, and many kinds of candy—aren't good for your body or your brain. Try to limit these kinds of foods. They clog your engine!

Complex carbohydrates. Your body also needs the nutrients found in complex carbohydrates, like breads, whole-wheat pasta (noodles), brown rice, and cereal.

Dealing with Food Sensitivities

Some parents of kids with ASD have reported that their children have sensitivities (reactions) to *gluten.* Gluten is found in products containing wheat, oats, barley, and other grains. Sensitivity to gluten can create problems with digestion and behavior. For this reason, these families may decide to go gluten-free. They carefully choose foods and drinks that don't contain any gluten at all, even trace amounts.

You still need to eat complex carbohydrates, even if you're on a gluten-free diet. Many grocery stores and special bakeries offer gluten-free breads, pizza crusts, bagels, muffins, and waffles. You can also find tasty pasta made from brown rice, corn, or potatoes.

Some families with children who have ASD also choose to go dairy-free. They have found that their kids do better if milk from cows is removed from their diet. So, products from dairy cows—like milk, butter, cheese, yogurt, and ice cream—are no longer allowed. All sorts of replacement products are available, though. For example, you can find milk made from soy, brown rice, or almonds. Dairy-free margarine is a good substitute for butter. Cheese and yogurt can be made from goat's milk or soy. If your regular grocery store doesn't carry these items, you can go to natural foods stores or order special foods online. It's essential to take calcium supplements if you go dairy-free because calcium helps build your bones.

Just because you have ASD doesn't mean you automatically have food sensitivities. And it doesn't mean you will do better if you're gluten- or dairy-free. But if you have ongoing problems with your digestion and seem to react to certain foods, your family can explore special diets as an option. Just be sure your doctor plays a role. You may want to see an allergy specialist or a dietician too.

Avoiding Dyes, Chemicals, and Sweeteners

Even if you don't go gluten- or dairy-free, it's important to watch your diet for foods and drinks that affect how you feel. Many kids with special needs react badly to foods with dyes that turn the food bright colors. The same is often true with foods containing chemicals called *preservatives* that help keep them fresh on the shelf or in the fridge. You should also avoid foods and drinks that use artificial sweeteners like the ones found in soda, sports drinks, and candy. Try to stay away from sugary treats and caffeine (found in coffee and cola drinks), because you'll probably feel jumpy and out of sorts.

What can you have instead? When you're in the mood for something sweet, try foods sweetened with honey, brown sugar, molasses, or stevia. Instead of soda, drink some fruit juice (not the kind sweetened with corn syrup). You can still bake cookies and other treats, even if they aren't made with gluten or dairy.

Choosing Healthy Foods Every Day

Changing your diet will mean making different choices at the school cafeteria. You might bring a lunch from home each day. If you're at a relative's home or visiting a friend, you'll probably need to take along your own snacks too. Then you'll be sure to

Take a Look!

Your doctor may tell you it's a good idea to take a multi-vitamin every day—one made especially for kids or teens (depending on your age). This will help ensure you get the nutrients you need. Vitamins come in all shapes, sizes, and flavors. You can find them in the form of a pill you chew (hard or soft), a pill you swallow, a liquid, or a powder you mix into foods or drinks. Try different ones to see what you like (but avoid ones with added dyes and chemicals).You can also ask about adding omega-3 fatty acids in the form of a "fish oil" pill, if you'd like. Experts believe that essential fatty acids help in brain development and overall health.

have something you can eat. If people ask why you eat the way you do, you can say, "I have sensitivities to certain foods." These days many kids have food allergies and sensitivities, so it's often no big deal to eat differently.

Choosing healthy foods is something your whole family can work on together. You can learn about the importance of:

- eating lots of fruits and veggies each day
- choosing healthy proteins and whole grains (found in whole-grain breads and cereals)
- avoiding too many packaged and "processed" foods (they have added chemicals)
- drinking lots of water to stay hydrated
- buying as many organic or fresh foods as possible
- consuming fewer foods that are high in fats, sugars, and sodium (salt)

In the end, you may find that a diet rich in fruits, vegetables, good proteins, and fresh ingredients helps you feel better overall. Your engine will run more smoothly and efficiently, and you'll be healthier!

What If You're a Choosy Eater?

Many kids who have ASD are very choosy about food . . . so choosy that they're often called "picky eaters."

Bella knows when her family's having pot roast for dinner. *Yuck*—the smell! The meat will be hard to chew, and there will be all those different vegetables swimming in the juices. She hates the smell *and* the taste. But she knows the rules. She has to take at least one bite of each food. Her parents stick to this rule because they're sure that someday Bella will learn to like new tastes and textures. So she does it—one bite of each. Then she's off to the fridge, where she finds her favorite food of all, mashed potatoes. She puts them in the microwave, and *beep*, they're ready! She sits at the table again, pleased she gets to make some choices about what she eats, even if it means following the rule about "one bite."

Danny loves all things salty. His favorite foods are French fries and potato chips. He would eat salty foods all day long, if only he was allowed. To him, one of the best parts of sharing a big bowl of popcorn with his family is licking all the salt off his fingers afterward. His parents have to watch to make sure Danny doesn't sneak salty foods when they're not looking.

Tameka has been having a hard time at lunch. The school cafeteria is always noisy and busy, and Tameka hates most of the foods that are served. She doesn't like crunchy foods or foods that smell too strong. This limits her choices. But now things are better: The school has agreed to let Tameka eat lunch in the special education room with her teacher. Tameka brings her lunch. She has whole-wheat macaroni and cheese along with peas that her grandma cooks just right for her. Her teacher heats up her lunch in the microwave. Now she can look forward to eating her favorite food in peace and quiet.

Breakfast is such a bother for **Levi.** He's supposed to be at the bus stop at 7:30, but he's hardly ever ready on time. The trouble is that it's really hard to get ready in the morning and eat breakfast too. Levi can't finish his cereal, and it's hard to try to sneak a piece of fruit on the bus. Levi's mom is worried he won't have enough energy if he doesn't eat breakfast. So she gives him a protein drink in a covered mug with a little opening in the lid. He gets special permission to drink this on the bus. Now he'll arrive at school fueled up and ready to learn.

Like Bella, Danny, Tameka, and Levi, maybe you're particular about what you eat and drink. Sensory issues are at the root of many problems with food. Usually what happens is something like this: You hate the texture (the way something feels) of certain foods in your mouth. You start gagging, or maybe even throw up a little. You remember that reaction. Then, the next time you see or smell the same food, you don't want it anywhere near your mouth! So, understandably, you refuse to eat it. Pretty soon, you resist other foods that remind you of the one you hated. That means whole categories of food are sometimes eliminated—no "mushy," no "hot," no "citrus," no "green."

If you're a picky eater, you know it's hard to learn to like things that seem horrible. Believe it or not, though, some food issues can be overcome. Learning to eat different things happens slowly. With lots of practice and patience, kids can learn to eat a wider variety of food—and enjoy it. Really!

How can you make that happen? Keep trying new foods, even if you're scared, disgusted, or convinced you can't do it. You can do it. Make it a goal to try one new food each week. If you hate it, okay . . . but don't cross that food off your list forever. A few months later, give that food another try, because you might decide you like it.

Your tastes change as you grow older, which means you'll learn to like more foods as time goes on. The same goes for sensitivities to textures. Over time, they tend to lessen, and that means you'll be able to try more things. An occupational therapist (OT) can help in this area.

However, your *family* is your greatest asset when it comes to changing how you eat. With their support and encouragement, you can make big or small adjustments to your diet. Keep trying and don't give up.

Chapter 23

Keeping It Clean (with Hygiene)

This chapter talks about the things that people often *don't* want to talk about. Embarrassing things, like how to stay fresh and clean. For example, you'll learn some basics about showers and baths, hair care, and hand washing. (All of that is part of hygiene.) But there's something else that's hard to talk about: the idea of looking like you're part of the crowd.

We hope you know that what's *inside* a person counts for way more than what's on the outside. Individuality is a great thing! In a perfect world, people would be accepted for who they are, no matter how they look or what they wear.

But the reality is that people *do* form opinions of you based on how you look. (It's not fair, but it's true.) Looking neat and clean can help you get along better with others. So can wearing clothes and shoes that are similar to what other kids your age wear. You don't have to spend a bunch of money on fashion, or dress in clothes you hate. It's a matter of finding what fits, feels comfortable, and "fits in."

Simple Steps for Success

Generally, kids with ASD show less interest in hygiene compared to other kids their age. Maybe that's true for you (or maybe it's not). If you start following some basic rules of hygiene at an early age, the tasks become easier and more automatic as you get older. Over time, you'll probably start adding more things to these hygiene basics, like shaving, putting on makeup, or even using contact lenses. For now all you need are some simple steps.

Maya's Story

Maya is 12 and tired of hearing about "puberty." Does her mom think that just because Maya has ASD she needs to hear about puberty every day? Her mom has explained that puberty means Maya is "growing up," and her body is changing. She's getting taller and needs to use deodorant so she doesn't have body odor. Maya understands this, but her mom seems to think Maya will forget or ignore her advice.

The worst thing for Maya is hearing her mom's comments about her hair. Maya has thick hair that's hard to wash. She used to wash her hair every three or four days, but now her mom says Maya should wash it more often or else it looks greasy.

Greasy? thinks Maya. *What does Mom think—that I rub* butter *in my hair?*

When Maya tries to wash her own hair, it's a big problem. It's really hard to figure out exactly how much shampoo to use. Too little shampoo means barely any lather. Too much shampoo means way too many suds. And rinsing seems to take forever.

Maya has tried adjusting the amount of shampoo she uses so that washing her hair won't be so frustrating. Her mom says, "Just use a *little* shampoo to wash your hair." This is confusing to Maya. How much is "a little"? Can't things be simpler or more clear? Some days, she goes to school feeling like there's extra shampoo in her hair. Her head feels itchy and icky. Other days, her mom says, "Maya, did you *really* wash your hair? Because it doesn't look like it got clean."

This morning, Maya gets up late for school. She runs to the shower and tries to rush, but then everything seems to go wrong. Her mom bought new shampoo, and it's in a huge, heavy bottle and smells too strong. When Maya opens the bottle, it slips from her hands and shampoo spills all over her.

Her mom calls, "Maya, we're going to be late if you don't hurry up!"

That's when the tears start. Maya hates everything: hair, showers, puberty. She wishes she could just go back to bed. Maya's mom sees how upset she is and helps out. Somehow they get to school on time.

Later, when Maya is back home, her mom says there's a surprise in the shower. Maya runs upstairs with her mom. When she opens the shower curtain, Maya sees a soap dispenser on the wall. It's like the ones near the sinks at school. "I don't get it, Mom," she says.

"Look!" her mom answers. Then she shows her a bottle of Maya's favorite scent-free shampoo and pours the whole thing into the dispenser. "All it takes is two pumps to get the amount you need. Try it."

Maya pumps the dispenser twice. The "right" amount of shampoo—not too much and not too little—appears in her palm.

"Wow, thanks, Mom!"

Now Maya knows that when she washes her hair, all she needs is "two pumps." That's easy to remember. Problem solved.

Bathe or shower each day. Depending on your age and abilities, you might still need some help washing up, or you may be doing just fine on your own. Try to take a bath or shower once a day or every other day, if possible. If you tend to be forgetful or have trouble completing tasks, ask a parent to create a waterproof checklist you can keep nearby when you wash. The checklist can include all the parts to wash, in which order, if you'd like. In the tub or shower, rinse yourself thoroughly to avoid itchy skin. Follow up with moisturizing lotion, if you want to.

Wash your hair as needed. Talk to a parent or another trusted adult about your hair-care needs. A lot depends on how long your hair is and whether it tends to be dry or oily. To keep it simple, you might want to get a shampoo that has a built-in conditioner. Try to notice when your hair looks greasy or flaky. These are signs that you need to wash it more frequently or use a different shampoo. Maybe you wonder if you should use gel or other styling products. You can get advice from a hairstylist or an older sister or brother.

Wash your face. Talk to an adult about how best to take care of your skin. Maybe all you need to do is wash your face with a cleanser. Or maybe you have some acne and need help taking care of pimples. Perhaps your skin is dry and you want to try a moisturizer. Have a parent spend time demonstrating the best way to take care of your skin. Then stick to a daily routine.

Wash your hands often. Keeping your hands clean helps prevent the spread of germs. Each time you wash, use warm water and lots of soap. Scrub for at least 30 seconds. That's long enough to sing the "ABC Song" (remember that?) in your head. Rinse well and dry your hands with a clean towel.

Hand-Washing Hints

Here are five good times to wash your hands:

1. before you eat

2. after using the bathroom

3. after you sneeze, cough, or blow your nose

4. after "gaming" (handheld games, video games, computer, etc.)

5. whenever they're dirty!

Brush and floss your teeth. Keeping your mouth healthy and clean starts with brushing at least twice a day. Two good times are after breakfast and before bed. Brush for two minutes, making sure to brush every tooth and your tongue. You can even buy a special rinse that helps you check out how well you brushed. If your teeth have colored spots after using the rinse, you missed a few places. Consider changing your toothbrush, if needed. Some kids who have ASD love electric vibrating toothbrushes. Others say they "can't stand" them—too much sensory input!

Floss every night too. Flossing takes some coordination. If it's hard for you, an adult can help. Or, you can try a toothpick-style flossing tool that has a handle to hold onto.

Deodorize as needed. Maybe you already need to use underarm deodorant, or maybe that's still a few years away. Use special foot powder if you sometimes have stinky, sweaty feet. If you hate stuff that has a heavy scent, choose unscented versions of hygiene products.

Take care of your nails. Fingernails and toenails need attention. But they're easy to forget about or overlook. Trim yours with a nail trimmer, file them with a nail file, or ask a parent for help in this area. This helps prevent hangnails and keeps your fingers and toes neater. If your nails are yellowed, you may have a fungus that requires medication. And if you're a nail biter, you might want to ask your doctor or a parent for some advice on how to stop this habit.

For every one of these hygiene tasks, making a checklist can help. Hang the checklist in a handy place, like on the bathroom mirror or behind the door.

Toothbrushing checklist:

☐ Use a pea-sized blob of toothpaste.

☐ Brush up and down. Use circular motions, like the dentist showed me.

☐ Brush for two minutes (use timer).

☐ Brush tongue.

☐ Rinse and spit.

☐ Make sure sink is clean afterward.

All in all, good hygiene leads to better health. So it's worth the extra work.

Looking Good Head to Toe

"Fashion" is tricky to talk about. In today's world, fashion videos and celebrities often make people think that looks, hair, and clothes are everything. Well, they aren't! So many other things are more important: kindness, courage, confidence, love for others, honesty, a giving spirit. The list goes on and on. You probably have many of these traits yourself. Way to go!

But here's the problem: Many kids, teens, and adults with ASD stand out because of what they wear. And not in a good way. We'd rather you stand out for your individuality, intelligence, sense of humor, or strong character. Those assets of yours will shine even brighter if you blend in when it comes to your clothing.

Does this mean you need to dress like a pop star or model to be accepted? No way! The tips in this chapter aren't meant to turn you into a dress-up doll or Mr. Trendy. You need to be yourself, and you've got to be comfortable. At the same time, it helps to look around and see if some of your clothing choices are giving people an impression you don't intend to give.

Dylan didn't know how to tie shoes. So he wore sneakers with Velcro when other boys in his class were wearing shoes with laces. For a long time, this didn't bother Dylan a bit. But then he noticed how much he liked some of the other sneaker styles. He wanted a pair for himself. But first, he'd need to learn to tie. Otherwise, what would happen at school if his laces came undone?

Selena loved leggings. They were easy to put on and didn't pinch like jeans. She had a drawer full of blue leggings that she wore winter and summer. One day a boy in her class said, "You wear the exact same pair of pants every day. That's *gross*." Selena knew he was rude, and wrong. She didn't wear the same exact pair—she had lots of different pairs. It wasn't like she pulled them out of the hamper every morning! But still, his comment bothered her.

Lionel hated buttons, snaps, and zippers. He preferred pants that had an elastic waistband, like sweatpants or sports pants. But Lionel often rushed as he got dressed. Then he'd forget to look in the mirror. His pants were usually twisted to the side, or pulled up really high. Some days he wore them backward or inside out.

Ellie was 12 but small for her age. She could still wear clothes in sizes meant for younger children. She loved princesses, so she almost always wore T-shirts and sweatshirts featuring Cinderella or Belle from *Beauty and the Beast*. Other girls in her class laughed at her for this.

Sometimes, it's a good idea to go beyond your usual clothing choices and s-t-r-e-t-c-h yourself to pick something new. Maybe "new" means tennies with laces or a pair of pants that zip. Maybe it means wearing T-shirts with different logos or images. Or making sure you're not wearing something that's too tight or small because you've outgrown it.

If you don't care a bit about fashion or clothes, that's fine. Maybe you're mostly concerned with what feels comfortable on your body. But you can be comfy *and* look "cool." What about getting someone who's interested in fashion to give you advice? (Tip: Choose someone your own age or just a little older.)

- **Look at magazines or clothing catalogs together.** You're probably a really visual person, so maybe some of the colors, styles, and choices will catch your eye. Ask your "fashion friend" what works and what doesn't. Talk about what might look good on you.

- **Go online.** If you don't like shopping in the store, you can shop online. (Do this with an adult's permission and supervision.) Look at kids' clothing stores or teen websites for ideas. If a parent orders your clothes online, you get to try them on in private at home, instead of in a public dressing room. Bonus!

- **Notice what other people your age wear.** Are certain brands and styles popular with your classmates or kids in your neighborhood? Find similar clothes at local stores or used-clothing shops. Maybe you have an older sibling or cousin who can hand down clothes to you.

- **Look in your own closet.** You might have more in there than you thought. Sometimes, it's easy to get into a habit of grabbing the first thing you see out of the closet or drawer, or picking something off the pile of folded laundry. If that's what you tend to do, you're probably wearing the same choices day after day. Try something else on instead. You might even ask your "fashion friend" to help you put together new outfits from what you already own.

Check Yourself Out

Before you head out the door each day, give yourself the "once-over":

Is your hair combed?

How are those teeth? Smile and say cheese! (Kidding.)

Is your shirt on the right way? (Not backward or inside out.)

Does your shirt need tucking in?

You're wearing clean underwear, right?

Does the outfit "go together"? Does it fit the season?

Belt buckled? Zipper up? Buttons done?

Are your pants, shorts, or skirt straight?

Do your socks match?

Are your laces tied?

Clothing may seem like an unimportant topic. After all, Einstein wasn't known as a snappy dresser, and look how far he went in life. Many creative people (like artists, writers, and musicians) dress either super-casual or weird-and-wacky—and they do just fine. Besides, you might think, "I'm just a kid in school. Who really cares what I wear for another day of math and gym?" These are all good points.

But one goal of this book is to help you find friends and feel good about yourself. If making some changes in what you wear and how you take care of yourself can help you succeed, then it's worth a try.

The tips in this chapter are a way to help you make little changes day to day. Take them step by step. In time, they may add up to big gains in confidence.

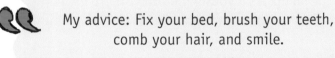

My advice: Fix your bed, brush your teeth, comb your hair, and smile.

—18-year-old boy

Chapter 24

Sleep . . . Zzzzzzz

Sleep time is *growing* time for kids and teens. You need a good night's rest every night to grow up healthy and feel good. But lots of kids on the autism spectrum have a hard time with sleep, for a variety of reasons.

Why do people need sleep in the first place? Lots of important functions take place while the body is at rest. For example:

- **You grow and heal.** Your body repairs and restores itself each night during sleep. As a young person you are growing. A lot of this growing happens at night when special hormones are released.

- **Your brain makes connections.** All the stuff you experience during the daytime is processed and stored in your memory. During sleep, your brain organizes this information and makes important connections with other parts of your brain. This helps your learning and your memory.

- **You save energy.** All day long your senses are on alert. You're seeing, hearing, tasting, touching, and smelling. At night while you sleep and dream, your senses get a much-needed break.

How much sleep is enough? The National Sleep Foundation says kids ages 6 to 13 need 9 to 11 hours of sleep per night. Teens need 8 to 10 hours. Not getting enough sleep night after night can lead to problems like these:

- being jittery and hyper
- decreased attention and short-term memory
- poorer performance in school and after-school activities

Plus, you just feel out of sorts when you're not getting enough sleep. That means your body doesn't work as well. You can get sick more easily, and you don't have as much energy. When your body is off-balance, so is your mind. You can't work as hard or think as well. Bad moods are a result, and no wonder! Who can be in a good mood when they're drowsy or feeling lousy?

Bedtime Basics

If you have trouble falling asleep or staying asleep, try some or all of the ideas here, depending on your needs.

Stay awake during the day. That may be hard for you, especially if you're a napper. But even a quick "catnap" can leave you rested enough that you may have trouble falling asleep at bedtime. If you nap, keep it short—have someone wake you up after 20 minutes so you can still fall asleep at bedtime.

Exercise. Physical activity is good for you for many reasons. One of those reasons is that you'll usually sleep better at night if your body is active during the day. Chapter 21 offers lots of ideas for getting exercise. Stay busy and active all day, but don't exercise right before bed. (It might perk you up instead of wearing you out.)

Have a bedtime routine. If you love routines, then setting up one for bedtime shouldn't be too difficult. A helpful routine includes time for relaxing, getting ready (putting on pajamas, washing up, brushing your teeth), and talking quietly with a loved one. Why spend time talking before bed? It gets your worries out and helps you relax. It also strengthens your relationships with people who care for you. If talking is hard, you can hold hands or hug.

Know your bedtime and stick to it. Talk to your dad or mom about what time you should go to bed. (The time depends on your age, what time school starts, how long it takes you to fall asleep and get ready in the morning, and what your parents think is best.) Once you have a bedtime, make sure you're in bed on time every night. This helps set your "body clock" so you're more likely to get sleepy at that time.

Avoid electronics at night. At least one hour before bed, turn off all electronics except for soothing music. That means no more TV, video games, computer or phone time, or loud, upbeat music. (All of these are stimulating—they give your body the "wake-up" signal.) Instead, do quiet activities like doodling, writing, or other suggestions that follow.

Take a long bath or a soothing shower. Hot or warm water can help you feel relaxed and sleepy. You might even want to add bath oil with chamomile or lavender to help you relax. Or, use a body wash that includes "relaxing" ingredients on the label.

Read. Reading is a quiet, soothing activity—unless you're into scary books (which aren't recommended before bed). Keep your favorite books within reach so they're a regular part of your bedtime routine. If reading is hard for you, ask a parent to read aloud to you. Or try audiobooks at a low volume, or choose books that are mostly pictures.

Breathe to relax. On page 188 is a Belly Breathing activity. You can also try the 10-step relaxation exercise on pages 188–189.

Get a rubdown. This is a good choice if you don't mind being touched, and you have a parent who's willing to give you a massage. Maybe you don't like deep pressure—so ask your dad or mom to lightly rub your back or tickle your arms. You can give yourself a foot massage too. Getting a foot or body rub can relax you and make you feel sleepy. (On the other hand, it might make you feel more awake! Try it during the daytime once or twice to see what effect it has.)

Watch what you eat and drink. If you drink a liquid with caffeine (like soda, coffee, or tea) in the late afternoon or evening, you'll probably have a harder time getting to sleep. The same goes for eating chocolate (which contains caffeine). Some people react to spicy foods. They may have trouble sleeping afterward or get bad dreams. Many people react to sugary foods and drinks too. They get a "sugar high" that's like fake energy, followed by a "crash" where they feel completely wiped out.

If you have any sleep problems, keep a log of what you eat or drink. That way you can find a pattern. It's also helpful to limit the liquids you drink after dinner. Then you're less likely to have to get up in the night to use the bathroom.

Use an alarm clock. Get up at the same time each morning. Set your alarm for a certain time. When it goes off, try to get up instead of pushing the snooze button a bunch of times. After getting up at the same time for a while, your body might automatically wake up just as your alarm is about to ring.

Darken the room. Maybe you're sensitive to light. Maybe you need a really dark room to sleep in. You can get curtains and room-darkening blinds. If this is true for you, keep all the lights off. Don't use a night-light if you can help it. You might also need to unplug any electronics that light up. (Find an alarm clock that lets you completely turn off the glowing numbers so they don't keep you awake.)

Keep it quiet. Ask your family to turn down the volume on any electronics that are still being used after you go to bed. See if they'll talk more softly and avoid making sudden noises, like slamming doors or banging around. If noise is really a problem for you, try some special headphones designed to block out sound. Or get some ear plugs from the drugstore. You may want to try a white-noise machine. It will create a repeating, soothing sound (like waves washing ashore or a train chugging along a track). Or, you can just use a fan.

Get comfortable. What helps you sleep? A pair of warm pajamas? Sleeping in only your underwear? Being tightly wrapped in blankets? Cotton sheets instead of flannel? People prefer different temperatures for sleeping. Check if you're too hot or cold, too weighed down or not snug enough. Try different types of pajamas to see what you like best. Maybe a nightgown gets too tangled, or long johns are too hot or tight. Wear only what's comfortable. Ask a parent to cut the labels off of your pajamas, so they don't rub against your skin.

Think about your pet. Does it help you sleep if your cat is right next to you or if your dog is on the floor by your bed? Then maybe that can be part of your routine. On the other hand, maybe your pet is waking you during the night. You might need to move your hamster or bird cage, for example, or shut the door so your pets can't come in.

Have a plan. What happens if you wake up during the night and have trouble falling back to sleep? Sometimes, just the *worry* of waking up makes sleep more difficult. It helps to have a plan in place. For example, if you wake up you might take a few sips of water, adjust the blankets, or turn over and try a different position. Try picturing and counting sheep in your head or letting your mind wander. If you start thinking stressful thoughts, stop and breathe. Hug your stuffed animals. Think about positive things, like what you're grateful for in life or who you love. Say a prayer. Do some deep breathing.

Stay in the bedroom. Some kids with ASD are very light sleepers. They wake up at night when the rest of the family is sleeping. If this is a problem for you, it's important to have a plan in place, so you're safe at home each night. It's best to stay in your room, even if you're wide awake and everyone else is asleep. Read a book or put on headphones and listen to soothing music. Try to stay calm and relaxed so you have a better chance of getting back to sleep.

One of the best ways you can help yourself get a better night's rest is to let people know how you're doing. Are you often too wound up to settle in to sleep? Do worries keep you awake? Do you get scared of the dark? Do you feel tired during school? Do you usually fall asleep on the bus? Do you crave more physical activity during the day?

First, you need to notice what feels "wrong" to you. Then you can communicate the problem to the adults you trust—a parent, your doctor, a counselor, or a therapist. For more on tuning into feelings or handling emotions, see Chapter 16.

Two Guys Want to Say

Remember at the beginning of the book, when we authors mentioned that our sons have autism? When the first edition of this book was published in 2012, Elizabeth Reeve's son Sam was age 25. Elizabeth Verdick's son Zach was 11. This updated edition of *The Survival Guide for Kids with Autism Spectrum Disorder* was created in 2021. (If you do the math, you'll know how old Zach and Sam are now.) Zach and Sam have personal insights into having ASD and wanted to share some of them with you here.

From Zach

ASD is difficult to manage. It often interferes with things that others seem to do naturally in life. But it's important to remember that you are gifted with unique and remarkable traits. You may have an incredible memory about the things you enjoy most—books, video games, or schoolwork. You may have difficulty expressing yourself and tend to struggle in social situations. But, because of this, it's likely that you'll become more empathetic, amiable, and maybe even a joy to be around.

In the vast sea of humanity, you are the current that pushes others forward—toward accepting what isn't typical. You serve as a reminder that all people can try to achieve their dreams, no matter what tries to stop them. I know this because I look at my own life and think about how far I've come from my challenging beginnings. When I was younger, I couldn't understand myself. I threw fits when things didn't go exactly as I wanted. The world wasn't going at my pace, so what I chose to do was set my own pace in the world and accept it. Now I have good grades. I am going to college and want to someday get a job.

So, remember: walk with your head held high, because you are a gift to this world.

From Sam

Autism is something that varies from person to person. How it affects one person is totally different from how it affects another. For me, it makes me really neurotic about checking to make sure I have everything I need. This sometimes really frustrates my mother. I also have to do some things in a very particular way. I get distracted very easily, and I have to really try to stay focused. Another thing I have to deal with is that my brain sometimes takes things too literally. This happens even when I know something was meant only in a general sense.

Although I get frustrated sometimes, my autism is part of what makes me who I am. I know that is how it will be for the rest of my life. Even with autism, I have made great progress over the years and have had many successes. Some of the things I am the proudest of include getting and keeping a job and finding ways to be successful in college. Balancing homework and a social life is hard as it is, but when you're much more easily distracted than others it's even harder. It took years for me to figure out the strategy that worked best for me.

I am very fortunate in that I have always had a very positive attitude about pretty much everything. So I will say this to you: Do not ever give up. Do not sit and think you will never be able to do something most people can do. It may take you much longer than other people, but you can do it. You absolutely can.

Before You Go

You've reached the end of this book. We hope it has given you some answers to questions you've wanted to ask, and maybe some you hadn't even thought of. This is the kind of book you and your parents can go back to again and again, whenever you need help. Share it with your brothers and sisters so they can understand you better. Share it with friends you think might need help on their own path.

As you get older, each day will bring new experiences—and more questions. Finding the answers won't always be easy. Remember to call on your "team" (Chapter 7). They're there for you in good times and not-so-good times. You can add more team members as the years go on.

Know what this is?

A label. The one-size-fits-all kind. At times, you might feel like a "label" because you have ASD. You might think you *are* your symptoms or your challenges. You are so much more than both!

There is no such thing as one-size-fits-all. Each of us is an individual. *You* are an individual—in life and on the spectrum too. No one can predict today who you'll be when you grow up.

One thing you might be is a "late bloomer." That means someone whose talents and capabilities are slower to develop. Many people, on the spectrum and not, are late bloomers. They still bloom! So keep learning. Keep reaching.

Yes, you will face frustrations. Life is full of hurts and hardships (for everyone). You'll get through them. And you know what? You'll be stronger for it. The hard times teach us to bend. They also teach us to try to help others through *their* hard times.

As life goes on, you can look forward to many other parts of the human experience: fun new friendships, wild laughter, excellent days, and feelings of "It's great to be alive."

Live life to the fullest. And let us know what happens.

Where to Go for More Info

It's easy to find websites about autism and life on the spectrum. Some of the sites offer medical information. Others are designed to help families learn about behavioral interventions and ways to cope with the diagnosis. And some sites are focused on including the voices of those on the spectrum and advocating for disability rights. Look online to see what interests you. Make sure the information on each site seems honest, authentic, and useful to you. Because websites come and go, we decided to make a list of suggested books that may interest you. Some of these books are written for teens, or even adults. If you don't feel ready for some, save them for when you *are* ready, as part of your own "autism library."

Nonfiction

Asperger's Rules!: How to Make Sense of School and Friends by Blythe Grossberg (Magination Press, 2012).

The Asperkid's (Secret) Book of Social Rules: The Handbook of Not-So-Obvious Social Guidelines for Tweens and Teens with Asperger Syndrome by Jennifer Cook O'Toole (Jessica Kingsley Publishers, 2012).

The Aspie Teen's Survival Guide: Candid Advice for Teens, Tweens, and Parents, from a Young Man with Asperger's Syndrome by J. D. Krause (Future Horizons, 2010).

Diary of a Young Naturalist by Dara McAnulty (Little Toller Books, 2020).

Freaks, Geeks & Asperger Syndrome: A User Guide to Adolescence by Luke Jackson (Jessica Kingsley Publishers, 2002).

Population One: Autism, Adversity, and the Will to Succeed by Tyler McNamer (Avia, 2013).

The Reason I Jump: The Inner Voice of a Thirteen-Year-Old Boy with Autism by Naoki Higashida, translated by KA Yoshida and David Mitchell (Random House, 2013).

Thinking in Pictures: My Life with Autism by Temple Grandin (Vintage, 2006). Her other books on autism include *The Autistic Brain* and *The Way I See It: A Personal Look at Autism & Asperger's*.

Fiction

Anything But Typical by Nora Raleigh Baskin (Simon & Schuster, 2009).

A Boy Called Bat by Elana K. Arnold (Walden Pond Press, 2017). Follow-up books include *Bat and the End of Everything* and *Bat and the Waiting Game*.

Colin Fischer by Ashley Edward Miller and Zack Stentz (Razorbill, 2012).

The Curious Incident of the Dog in the Night-Time by Mark Haddon (Doubleday, 2003). This story was eventually turned into a play.

Get a Grip, Vivy Cohen! by Sarah Kapit (Dial, 2020).

The London Eye Mystery by Siobhan Dowd (Yearling, 2009).

Marcelo in the Real World by Francisco X. Stork (Arthur A. Levine Books, 2009).

Me and Sam-Sam Handle the Apocalypse by Susan Vaught (Paula Wiseman, 2020).

Mindblind by Jennifer Roy (Skyscape, 2013).

Mockingbird by Kathryn Erskine (Philomel, 2010).

Rain Reign by Ann M. Martin (Feiwel and Friends, 2014).

The Real Boy by Anne Ursu (Walden Pond Press, 2013).

Rules by Cynthia Lord (Scholastic, 2008).

The Someday Birds by Sally J. Pla (HarperCollins, 2017).

The State of Grace by Rachael Lucas (Feiwel and Friends, 2017).

The Strange Case of Origami Yoda by Tom Angleberger (Abrams, 2010). There's now an eight-book box set of titles in the series. For more about this author, see page 33.

A Whole New Ballgame: A Rip and Red Book by Phil Bildner (Farrar, Straus & Giroux, 2015). There are other Rip and Red follow-up titles, such as *Rookie of the Year* and *Tournament of Champions*.

A Word About ASD Characters

Most of the fiction books included in this list are written by people who don't have ASD, but their characters *do*. These books are works of the imagination—an exploration of character and difference. They're not meant to represent everyone on the spectrum. There's no way they could.

If you read any of these books, ask yourself if you think the portrayal of a young person with ASD feels authentic to you or not. Does the character seem relatable? Heroic? Stereotypical? Does the individual seem to be a collection of symptoms or odd behaviors? How does the character struggle—how do others around the character struggle? How does the person on the spectrum change and grow?

Now that it's more common to see such characters in literature, in movies, and on TV, people have greater knowledge about ASD. But guess what? People still have misconceptions about ASD. They simply can't understand it as well as someone who's on the spectrum. Someone like *you*. You can let your own voice be heard—in the real world and in terms of artistic expression. Maybe you'll write, maybe you'll act, maybe you'll sing. Add *your* words to the mix!

Sharing the Diagnosis with Your Child
(For Parents)

It's not an easy decision to tell your child about the diagnosis. So many questions crop up . . . *How do I tell him? What are the "right" words? Will she understand? Is there a certain age kids should be told? Will telling my child affect his confidence and self-esteem? Where should the conversation take place—at home? During therapy? At the doctor's office? What if the conversation doesn't go well—then what?*

One of the reasons we wrote this book was so you could use it as part of the process of getting the conversation started.

There is no tried-and-true way to tell your child about the diagnosis, but you can do several things to make the conversation go more smoothly. First and foremost, know that it's likely your child is already aware of being "different" in some way. The news may not be as shocking as you think. Kids with autism spectrum disorder realize they struggle in certain areas, but they don't know why. They may think, "I do everything wrong" or "It's all my fault." They may wonder why they're in a special education program or why they see doctors and therapists a lot more often than other kids do. When you talk to your child about autism, it's an opportunity for you to give not only the reasons but also *reassurance.* Children need to know that having the condition isn't their fault.

The most important thing you can do is to keep the conversation positive. Wait until you yourself are at a point of acceptance. If you're not sure the diagnosis is correct or if you're feeling depressed, angry, or anxious, the timing isn't yet right. Your child will most likely be aware of your confusion and sadness and may return to thinking, "I do everything wrong" or "It's all my fault."

How do you keep the conversation positive? By making it clear that you're there to answer questions, to offer support, and to always be a source of unconditional love. Point out your child's many strengths, rather than focusing on weaknesses. Show empathy. And remember to tell your child, "I'm so proud of you."

Here are tips to start the conversation and keep it going:

Look for signs of readiness. Is your child asking questions such as, "Why do I have to go to therapy?" or "How come other kids aren't like me?" Have you heard your child say something like, "I'm so stupid!" or "I can't do things right"? These are signals that your child already senses a difference.

Choose a good time. You may want to wait until your home is quiet and your child is calm. You could talk during a weekend, when after-school activities and homework aren't a pressing issue. Don't have the conversation on a "bad day"—for example, after your child has had an outburst or a meltdown, scored poorly on a test, or gotten into an argument with a friend. Pick a time when all is (relatively) well.

Have a plan in place. Decide ahead of time who will do the telling. Will it be you? Your spouse or partner? Do you want other trusted people on hand, such as your child's doctor or therapist, or special family members like grandparents and older siblings? Think about who your child is most comfortable around and what role others might play in the discussion.

Make the conversation age-appropriate. You can keep things simple for younger kids or go more in-depth for older ones. Use *The Survival Guide* as needed; read a chapter or two aloud, or show the book and explain that it is a tool for understanding when your child is ready to learn more.

Be conscious of how your child responds. If your child shows signs of distress, end the conversation. Let your child know you can talk later, and then allow some space and private time. Open the door to questions when your child feels ready.

Know the facts. Autism spectrum disorder is considered a medical condition. Kids who have ASD need help, guidance, and support. Some parents make the mistake of believing that because a diagnosis will lead to a label, that label will then hold their child back in school, in social situations, and throughout life. But failing to acknowledge the condition doesn't change the reality of it. Other parents attempt to soften the truth by telling children they have a learning disorder or a developmental delay. This terminology may give children the impression that they'll outgrow the problem or "get better" if they "do things right." Avoiding the diagnosis or giving it a different name only postpones the process of getting kids the help they need and deserve.

Your child has a better chance of succeeding in life if you face the diagnosis with an open mind, an open heart, and firmer footing on the path ahead.

Sources of Facts and Quotations

Pages 14 and 28: *Freaks, Geeks & Asperger Syndrome: A User Guide to Adolescence* by Luke Jackson. Jessica Kingsley Publishers, 2002, pages 19 and 35, and page 44.

Page 26: *Emergence: Labeled Autistic (A True Story)* by Temple Grandin and Margaret M. Scariano. Warner Books, 1986, page 22.

Page 27: *Autism. An Inside-Out Approach* by Donna Williams. Jessica Kingsley Publishers, 1996.

Page 30: *Autism Spectrum Quarterly,* "An Interview with Rudy Simone," by Liane Holliday Willey, Ed.D., summer 2010, page 45.

Page 34: "How Asperger's Powers My Writing" by Tom Angleberger, in *The Guardian,* April 8, 2015, theguardian.com/childrens-books-site/2015/apr/08 aspergers-writing-autism-awareness-origami-yoda -tom-angelberger.

Page 39: The information from the study of twins was reported in "Genetics Less Important than Environment in Understanding, Curing Autism, Study Says" by Andy Hinds, July 5, 2011, reporting on a study analyzing the frequency of autism in 192 pairs of twins conducted by the University of California–San Francisco and Stanford and described in the *Archives of General Psychiatry.* Accessed November 18, 2011, at Discovery Communications' TLC Parentables (parentables.howstuffworks.com) under "Health and Wellness."

Page 42: "A Journey Through Autism" by Max LaZebnik, in *The Autism Perspective (TAP)* Magazine, January–March 2005, page 36.

Page 42: *How to Talk to an Autistic Kid* by Daniel Stefanski. Free Spirit Publishing, 2011, pages 30 and 41.

Page 51: *A Friend Like Henry: The Remarkable Story of an Autistic Boy and the Dog That Unlocked His World* by Nuala Gardner. Sourcebooks, 2008, pages 251–252.

Page 56: The "Manners Words" chart is adapted from *Dude, That's Rude! (Get Some Manners)* by Pamela Espeland and Elizabeth Verdick. Free Spirit Publishing, 2007, page 4. Used with permission.

Page 62: "6 Tips for Being a Good Sport with Family Members" is adapted from *Siblings: You're Stuck with Each Other, So Stick Together* by James J. Crist and Elizabeth Verdick. Free Spirit Publishing, 2010, pages 98–100. Used with permission.

Pages 64–65: The "STOP THINK GO" strategy is adapted from *Don't Behave Like You Live in a Cave* by Elizabeth Verdick. Free Spirit Publishing, 2010, pages 55–56. Used with permission.

Pages 82 and 161: "Looking You in the Mouth: Abnormal Gaze in Autism Resulting from Impaired Top-Down Modulation of Visual Attention" by Dirk Neumann et al, in *Oxford Journals, Social and Cognitive & Affective Neuroscience,* 2006, Volume 1, Issue 3, pages 194–202.

Page 127: *The Aspie Teen's Survival Guide: Candid Advice for Teens, Tweens, and Parents, from a Young Man with Asperger's Syndrome* by J.D. Kraus. Future Horizons, 2010, pages 151–152.

Pages 187–188: Belly breathing instructions are adapted from *Be the Boss of Your Stress* by Timothy Culbert and Rebecca Kajander. Free Spirit Publishing, 2007, pages 30–31. Used with permission.

Pages 188–189: The relaxation exercise is adapted from *Stress Can Really Get on Your Nerves* by Trevor Romain and Elizabeth Verdick. Free Spirit Publishing, 2018, pages 75–76. Used with permission.

Pages 203–207: The "Check Your Engine" section is adapted from *Don't Behave Like You Live in a Cave* by Elizabeth Verdick. Free Spirit Publishing, 2010, pages 86–92. Used with permission of Free Spirit. The engine concept is introduced in *How Does Your Engine Run?* by Mary Sue Williams and Sherry Shellenberger. Albuquerque: Therapy Works, 1996.

Page 224: Information on how much sleep is enough comes from the National Sleep Foundation.

Index

About the Authors

In her role as a child and adolescent psychiatrist, Dr. Elizabeth Reeve has worked with children, teens, and adults on the autism spectrum for more than 30 years. She is also the mother of a young man with autism. As a parent and physician, she experiences the day-to-day challenges of ASD at home and at work. Dr. Reeve recalls that at various times she was told her own child was "hard of hearing" and "intellectually disabled" (although he wasn't), and that he "may never walk" or "could go blind" (wrong again). Today, as an adult, he works part-time, has an active social life, enjoys many hobbies, and loves taking classes to further his education. He attends college. The struggles were many, but hard work continues to pay off.

Elizabeth Verdick writes from the perspective of a mother with a child on the spectrum too. Advocating for her son since he was two years old has been one of the greatest learning experiences in her life. Along the way, she has worked with doctors, behavioral therapists, teachers, school counselors, and speech, occupational, and physical therapists to help her son. As an author of many books for children and teens, she knew she'd someday want to write a book for her son and other kids like him in the hope that it may be a guide to help them not only survive, but *thrive.* Many of her books for kids of all ages address SEL (social and emotional learning) and behavioral issues. Learn more about her work at **elizabethverdick.com.**